The Wisdom of
THE KABBALAH

The Wisdom of
THE KABBALAH

As represented by chapters taken from the book Zohar

With a Foreword by
Dagobert D. Runes

PHILOSOPHICAL LIBRARY

CITADEL PRESS
Kensington Publishing Corp.
www.kensingtonbooks.com

The body of the Zohar text was taken, with only essential revisions, from the English translation by S. L. MacGregor Mathers. The English version, entitled *The Kabbalah Unveiled* (Routledge and Kegan Paul), is based on the Latin edition of Knorr von Rosenroth, and collated with the original Chaldee and Hebrew text.

CITADEL PRESS books are published by Kensington Publishing Corp., 850 Third Avenue, New York, NY 10022. Citadel Press and its logo are trademarks of Kensington Publishing Corp.

Titles included in the Wisdom Library are published by arrangement with Philosophical Library.

All Kensington titles, imprints, and distributed lines are available at special quantity discounts for bulk purchases for sales promotions, premiums, fund raising, educational, or institutional use. Special book excerpts or customized printings can also be created to fit specific needs. For details, write or phone the office of the Kensington special sales manager: Kensington Publishing Corp., 850 Third Avenue, New York, NY 10022, attn: Special Sales Department, phone 1-800-221-2647.

First Wisdom Library printing May 2001

10 9 8 7 6 5 4 3 2 1

Printed in the United States of America

Cataloging data for *The Wisdom of the Kabbalah* may be obtained from the Library of Congress.

ISBN 0-8065-2249-6

CONTENTS

FOREWORD

The present selection is taken from *Sepher ha-Zohar, The Book of Splendor,* written about 1300 in Spain. It is the only piece of post-talmudic literature that was to be used by many as a text, almost equal to the Torah and Talmud. The *Zohar* was and still is the classical expression of Jewish mysticism.

Like the Midrash, it is written in a homiletical manner, following the Platonic style of attributing dominance in the dialogues to the Socratic Rabbi Simeon Ben Yochai.

Kabbalah is that great body of Hebrew literature that sprang up and grew parallel to the traditional writings of rabbinical literature, for a period of over a thousand years. Its origins are clouded in uncertainty, its authors doubtful or anonymous, and its forms of expression varied as they are unusual.

Kabbalah signifies "receiving." However, only few were given the inner light by which they could behold the visions of eternity. The secret doctrines concerning God are revealed to the spiritually prepared only.

In a sense, the Kabbalah was a silent protest movement of the mystic element against formalism; a role which it played not only in Judaism but also in Christian Protestantism (Reuchlin a.o.).

The great theme of the Kabbalah is God before creation, and the soul of man after it.

God is *ain soph,* the endless, ever creating; or, in the words of the great philosopher of Mysticism, Baruch Spinoza, *"Natura naturans"* (infinite creative substance).

God manifests Himself in ten emanations, or *Sephiroth*. His divine attributes are: Wisdom, Reason, Knowledge, Greatness, Strength, Beauty, Eternity, Majesty, Principle, and Sovereignty *(Chokmah, Binah, Daath, Gedulah, Geburah, Tiphereth, Netzach, Hod, Yesod, Malkuth)*.

Man is part of this created world, but man is also given to glory in the emanations of the heavens. Man can lift the curtain of the great Unknown and raise himself into the abode of the blessed spirit by dedicating his life to *Chabad* (Wisdom, Reason, Knowledge), the first three of the Divine Emanations.

This sublime love of the Divine transcends physical being and transforms mere man into the *Zaddik*, the Righteous One, who, seeing the inner stream of creation, lives in the bliss of fundamental faith and equanimity. His body is earthly but his soul is of the heavens. He is united with God in a mystical union which can be comprehended by the initiated only *(Yihud)*.

Again we are reminded of Spinoza and his theorem, "The love of man to God and the love of man to man are one and the same."

The Kabbalah, although offering no moral regulative or system of precepts, is inherently a philosophy of ethics. Its writings may point to examination of the symbolic meaning of the Hebrew alphabet; they may encourage a semanticism based on initials and numbers; they may become involved with incarnation and magic, with amulets and spiritism, demonology, exorcism, or Messianism; the essence of the Kabbalah has ever been man's mystical union with God in thoughts of wisdom and deeds of kindness.

The literature of the Kabbalah has its beginning in Palestine and Babylon in the post-talmudic era. Of the systematic books of the early epoch are *Shiur Komah*, dealing with the measures of God, and *Sepher Yetzirah*, Book of Creation.

In the early middle ages the center of Kabbalist study moved from the Middle East to the Mediterranean countries and Germany. The major works of that era are *Masechet Azilut*, a treatise on emanations; *Sepher ha-Bahir*, the Book of Enlightenment; *Sepher ha-Temunah*, the Book of the Image; and last and foremost, the *Zohar*, or Splendor.

The *Zohar is* generally and rightly regarded as the main work of the Kabbalah. It was written in Aramaic in the manner of a commentary to the Torah. It was composed and published toward the end of the thirteenth century by Moses ben Shemtov de Leon, of Castile (d. 1305).

In the sixteenth century the center of Kabbalah veered back to Palestine, especially the city of Safed. Its great representatives were Moses Cordovero, the profound theoretician of Kabbalism; Isaac Luria, the Saint; and his disciple Hayim Vital, who put his master's teachings on paper.

The Safed school of Kabbalah became a source of great inspiration to the fervent religious movements of Eastern Europe of the later centuries, culminating in the tremendously powerful revival movement of Jewish mysticism in the eighteenth and nineteenth centuries, known as Chassidism.

Founded by Rabbi Israel ben Eliezer (1700–1760), called Baal Shem Tov, Master of the Good Name, Chassidism (Pietism) is based on the application of kabbalistic principles of union with God. Its emphasis is on the guidance of the Zaddikim, the righteous, and constant direct communion with the Heavens.

The Kabbalah in all its ways and byways is based on the theology of *Schechinah*, God's indwelling in man.

Man can reach the Divine in his own heart, in his own faith.

Man can reach the Divine in meditation of the oneness and infiniteness of the Lord.

Man can reach the Divine in deeds of kindness, as love to man is but love to God in another form. Man's destiny is the practice of *Tikkun*, to restore harmony to the world by spreading God's scattered light into every corner.

The Kabbalah is called the third of the great literatures in the Hebrew faith, next to the Bible and Talmud. Indeed, they are all three but one. And if some may point out that not always did holy wisdom guide the scriptural text, it is not difficult to pull back the frilly curtain of the incidental and gaze upon the celestial splendor of what is forever the Faith of Israel.

D. D. R.

The Wisdom of
THE KABBALAH

THE GREATER HOLY ASSEMBLY

CHAPTER I

PREFACE

1. TRADITION.—Rabbi Schimeon spake unto his companions, and said: "How long shall we abide in the condition of one column by itself? when it is written, Ps. cxix, 126: 'It is time for Thee, Lord, to lay to Thine hand, for they have destroyed Thy law.'

2. "The days are few, and the demandor is urgent; the herald crieth aloud daily, and the reapers of the land are few; and those who are about the end of the vineyard attend not, and have not known where may be the lawful place. *(That is, do not study holiness, which is called the vineyard.)*

3. "Assemble yourselves, O my companions, in an open space, equipped with armor and spears; be ye ready in your preparations, in council, in wisdom, in understanding, in science, in care, with hands and with feet! Appoint as King over you, Him in whose power is life and death so that the words of truth may be received: things unto which the supernal holy ones attend, and rejoice to hear and to know them."

4. Rabbi Schimeon sat down and wept; then he said: "Woe! if I shall reveal it! Woe! if I shall not reveal it!"

5. His companions who were there were silent.

6. Rabbi Abba arose and said unto him: "With the favor of the Lord, also it is written, Ps. xxv, 14: 'The Arcanum of the Lord is with them that fear Him.' And well do these companions fear that Holy and Blessed One; and now they have entered into the assembly of the tabernacle of his house, some of them have only entered, and some of them have departed also."

7. Moreover, it is said the companions who were with Rabbi Schimeon were numbered, and they were found to consist of Rabbi Eleazer, his son; and Rabbi Abba, and Rabbi Yehuda, and Rabbi Yosi the son of Jacob, and Rabbi Isaac, and Rabbi Chisqiah the son of Rav, and Rabbi Chiya, and Rabbi Yosi, and Rabbi Yisa.

8. They gave their hands unto Rabbi Schimeon, and raised their fingers on high, and entered into a field under the trees and sat down.

9. Rabbi Schimeon arose and offered up a prayer. He sat in the midst of them, and said: "Let whosoever will place his hand in my bosom." They placed their hands there, and he took them.

10. When he began, he said (from Deut. xxvii, 15): "Cursed be the man that maketh any graven or molten image, the work of the hands of the craftsman, and putteth it in a secret place. And all the people shall answer and say Amen!"

11. Rabbi Schimeon began, and said: "Time for Thee, O Lord to lay to Thine hand." Why is it time for the Lord to lay to His hand? Because they have perverted Thy law. What is this, 'they hath perverted Thy law'? The higher law, which is itself made void, if it be not carried out according

to his commands. Wherefore is this? *(Or, as others read: Wherefore is this name Lord here employed?)* This hath been said concerning the Ancient of Days.[1]

12. "For it is written, Deut. xxxiii), 29: 'Blessed art thou, O Israel: who is like unto thee?' Also it is written, Exod. xv, 11: 'Who is like unto thee among the gods, O Lord?' "[2]

13. He called Rabbi Eleazer, his son, and commanded him to sit down before him, and Rabbi Abba on the other side, and said: "We are the type of all things" (that is, "we represent the three columns of the Sephiroth"); "thus far are the columns established."

14. They kept silence, and they heard a voice; and their knees knocked one against the other with fear. What was that voice? The voice of the Higher Assembly, which had assembled above. *(For out of Paradise came the souls of the just thither, that they might hearken, together with the Schechinah of the Presence Divine.)*

15. Rabbi Schimeon rejoiced, and said: "O Lord! I have heard Thy speech, and was afraid! (Hab. iii, i.) He hath said: 'It is therefore rightly done, seeing that fear hath followed; but for us the matter rather dependeth upon love.' Like as it

[1] *I.e.*, one of the names of Macroprosopus, the first emanation, the crown, Kether.

[2] In the above verse it is well to note that by Notariqon, the second division of the Literal Qabalah, the initial letters of the first quotation give the word *Aimakh*, "Thy terror," the addition of the numeration of which by Gematria, the first division of the Literal Qabalah, is 71; and that in a similar manner from the second quotation, the word *Maccabee*, is obtained, whose numeration is 72. Now, 72 is the number of the Schemahamphorasch, or "divided name," to which Maccabee is always referred. And if to the 71 of the first quotation we add A, expressing thus the hidden unity, we obtain 72 again. Furthermore, it is well to note that each quotation consists of four words, thus answering to the letters of the Lord. —Trans.

is written, Deut. vi, 5: 'And thou shalt delight in Lord thy God.' Also it is written, Mal. i, 2: 'I have loved you.' "

16. Rabbi Schimeon said further: " 'He who walketh, going up and down *(from one house unto another)* revealeth the secret; but the faithful in spirit concealeth the word' (Prov. xi, 13).

17. "'He who walketh going up and down.' This saying meriteth question, because it is said, 'going up and down.' Wherefore then 'walketh'? The man is already said to be going up and down: what is this word 'walketh'?

18. "For truly it is true concerning that man who is not stable in his spirit nor truthful, that the word which he hath heard is moved hither and thither, like a straw in the water, until it cometh forth from him.

19. "For what reason? Because his spirit is not a firm spirit.

20. "But concerning him who is firm in spirit it is written: 'But the faithful in spirit concealeth the word.' *(But this phrase)* 'faithful in spirit' denoteth firmness of spirit; like as it is said, Isa. xxii, 23: 'And I will fasten him as a nail in a sure place.' Matter dependeth upon Spirit.

21. "And it is written, Eccles. v, 6: 'Suffer not thy mouth to cause thy flesh to sin.'

22. "For neither doth the world remain firm, except through secrecy. And if in worldly affairs there be so great need of secrecy, how much more in the things of the most secret of secrets, and in the meditation of the Ancient of Days,[3] which matters are not even revealed unto the highest of the angels."

23. Rabbi Schimeon said, moreover: "I will not say it unto the heavens, that they may hear; I will not declare it unto

[3] Macroprosopus, the first Sephira.

the earth, that it may hear; for certainly we are (the symbols of) the pillars of the Universe."

24. It is said in the Arcanum of Arcana, that when Rabbi Schimeon opened his mouth, the whole place was shaken, and his companions also were shaken.

CHAPTER II

OF THE CONDITION OF THE WORLD OF VACANCY

25. HE manifested the Arcanum, and commencing, said, Gen. xxxvi, 29: "And those art the kings which reigned in the land of Edom before that a king could rule over the children of Israel."

26. Blessed are ye, O just men! because unto you is manifested the Arcanum of the Arcana of the law, which hath not been manifested unto the holy superior ones.

27. Who can follow out this matter? and who is worthy to do so? For it is the testimony of the truth of truths. Therefore let all our prayers be undertaken with devotion, lest it be imputed *(to me)* as a sin, that I am making this matter manifest.

28. And perchance my companions may speak unto me, because some objection may arise against these words. For truly this work is not such a one as may be easily written down, so that by it may appear how many kings there were before the children of Israel came, and before there was a king over the children of Israel: how therefore doth this matter agree? And for this reason my companions have moved the question.

29. Therefore the Arcanum of Arcana is what men can neither know nor comprehend, nor can they apply their rules of science to it.

30. It is said that before the Ancient of the Ancient Ones, the Concealed One of the Concealed Ones, instituted the formations of the King *(under certain members and paths of*

Microprosopus) and the diadems of the diadems *(that is, the varied coverings whereby the superfluity of the Lights is circumscribed)*; beginning and end existed not *(that is, there was neither communication nor reception).*

31. Therefore He carved out *(that is, hollowed out a space by which he might flow in)* and instituted proportions in Himself *(in as many ways as the Lights of His Understanding could be received, whence arose the paths of the worlds),* and spread out before Him a certain veil *(that is, produced a certain nature, by which His infinite light could be modified, which was the first Adam)*; and therein carved out and distributed the kings and their forms by a certain proportion *(that is, all creatures under a condition of proper activity; by which He Himself might be known and loved)*; but they did not subsist. *(Here is intimated the fall of the creatures, partly into a condition of quiet, such as matter; partly into a state of inordinate motion, such as that of the evil spirits.)*

32. That is the same thing which is said, Gen. xxxvi, 29: "And these are the kings which reigned in the land of Edom, before that there reigned a king over the children of Israel." The first king in respect of the children of Israel *(by the children of Israel are understood the paths of the restored world)* is the first.

33. And all those things which were carved out, but subsisted not, are called by their names *(that is, were divided into certain classes),* neither yet did they subsist, until He forsook them *(so that they could receive the lights from the receptacles above themselves),* and hid Himself before them (in diminished light).

CHAPTER III

CONCERNING THE ANCIENT ONE, OR MACRO-PROSOPUS, AND CONCERNING HIS PARTS, AND ESPECIALLY CONCERNING HIS SKULL

34. AND after a certain time was that veil entirely disunited in formless separation, and recomposed according to its conformation.

35. And this is the tradition: The Absolute desired within Himself to create the essence of light *(the law—that is, the letters of the alphabet, from whose transpositions the law was formed)*, hidden for two thousand years, and produced Her. And She answered thus unto Him: "He who wisheth to dispose and to constitute other things, let Him first be disposed according unto a proper conformation."

36. This is the tradition described in the "Concealed Book of the King,"[1] that the Ancient of the Ancient Ones, the Concealed of the Concealed Ones, hath been constituted and prepared as in various members *(for future knowledge)*.

37. Like as if it were said, "He is found (that is, He may in some way to a certain extent be known), and He is not found;" for He cannot be clearly comprehended; but He hath as it were been formed; neither yet is He to be known of any, since He is the Ancient of the Ancient Ones.

38. But in his conformation is He known; as also He is the Eternal of the Eternal Ones, the Ancient of the Ancient Ones, the Concealed of the Concealed Ones; and in His symbols is He knowable and unknowable.

[1] The "Siphra Dtzenioutha," chap. i § 16.

39. White are His garments, and His appearance is the likeness of a Face vast and terrible.

40. Upon the throne of flaming light is He seated, so that He may direct its (flashes).

41. Into forty thousand superior worlds the brightness of the skull of His head is extended, and from the light of this brightness the just shall receive four hundred worlds in the world to come.

42. This is that which is written, Gen. xxiii, 16: "Four hundred shekels of silver, current money with the merchant."

43. Within His skull exist daily thirteen thousand myriads of worlds, which draw their existence from Him, and by Him are upheld.

CHAPTER IV

Concerning the Dew, or Moisture of the Brain, of the Ancient One, or Macroprosopus

44. AND from that skull distilleth a dew upon Him which is external, and filleth His head daily.

45. And from that dew which floweth down from His head, that *(namely)* which is external, the dead are raised up in the world to come.

46. Concerning which it is written, Cant. v, 2: "My head is filled with dew." It is not written: "It is full with dew"; but *Nimla*, "it is filled."

47. And it is written, Isa. xxvi, 19: "The dew of the lights is Thy dew." Of the lights—that is, from the brightness of the Ancient One.

48. And by that dew are nourished the holy supernal ones.

49. And this is that manna which is prepared for the just in the world to come.

50. And that dew distilleth upon the ground of the holy apple trees. This is that which is written, Exod. xvi, 14: "And when the dew was gone up, behold upon the face of the desert a small round thing."

51. And the appearance of this dew is white, like unto the color of the crystal stone, whose appearance hath all colors in itself. This is that which is written, Num. xi, 7: "And its varieties as the varieties of crystal."

CHAPTER V

FURTHER CONCERNING THE SKULL OF MACROPROSOPUS

52. THE whiteness of this skull shineth in thirteen carved out sides: in four sides from one portion; in four sides from the part of His countenance; and in four sides from another part of the periphery; and in one above the skull, as if this might be called the supernal side.[1]

53. And thence is the Vastness of His Countenance extended into three hundred and seventy myriads of worlds; and hence *Arikh Aphim*,[2] Vastness of Countenance is His name.

54. And He Himself, the Most Ancient of the Most Ancient Ones, is called *Arikh Da-Anpin*, the Vast Countenance, or Macroprosopus; and He Who is more external is called *Zauir Anpin*, or Him Who hath the Lesser Countenance *(Microprosopus)*, in opposition to the Ancient Eternal Holy One, the Holy of the Holy Ones.

55. And when Microprosopus looketh back upon Him,

[1] The hidden sense of this somewhat obscure passage is, that the brightness arises from the skull, *which it conceals*, which latter is therefore the emblem of the Concealed One. The thirteen parts are three tetragrammatic forms, which give twelve letters, and symbolize thus the Trinity of the Tetragram; and the one supernal part is the unity. The meaning therefore is, the Trinity in Unity, proceeding from the Concealed Unity, which also proceedeth from the Negatively Existent. Thirteen, moreover, occultly points out unity, for *Achad,* Unity, adds up for thirteen.

[2] Or, *Aurikha Da-Anpin*, the Vast Countenance.

all the inferiors are restored in order, and His Countenance is extended, and is made more vast at that time, but not for all time *(then only is it)*, vast like unto the *(countenance)* of the More Ancient one.

56. And from that skull issueth a certain white shining emanation, toward the skull of Microprosopus, for the purpose of fashioning His head; and thence toward the other inferior skulls, which are innumerable.

57. And all the skulls reflect this shining whiteness toward the Ancient of Days,[3] when they are numbered out of their mingled confusion. And by reason of this there existeth herein an opening toward the skull below, when they proceed to numeration.

---

[3] Macroprosopus.

CHAPTER VI

Concerning the Membrane of the Brain of Macroprosopus

58. In the hollow of the skull is the aerial membrane of the supreme hidden Wisdom, which is nowhere disclosed; and it is not found, and it is not opened.

59. And that membrane enshroudeth the brain of the hidden Wisdom, and therefore is that Wisdom covered, because it is not opened through that membrane.

60. And that brain, which is itself the hidden Wisdom, is silent and remaineth tranquil in its place, like good wine upon its lees.

61. And this is that which they say:—Hidden is the science of the Ancient One, and His brain is calm and concealed.

62. And that membrane hath an outlet toward Microprosopus, and on that account is His brain extended, and goeth forth by thirty and two paths.[1]

63. This is that same thing which is written: "And a river went forth out of Eden" (Gen. ii, 7). But for what reason? Because the membrane is *(then)* opened, neither doth it *(completely)* enshroud the brain.

64. Nevertheless the membrane is opened from below. And this is that which we have said: Among the signatures of the letters *(is) Tau*, TH; nevertheless He impresseth it as

---

[1] Which are the thirty-two paths of the *Sepher Yetzirah,* or Book of Formation; symbolized by the ten numbers and twenty-two letters of the Hebrew alphabet.

the sign of the Ancient of Days, from Whom dependeth the perfection of knowledge, because He is perfect on every side, and hidden, and tranquil, and silent, like a good wine upon its lees.

CHAPTER VII

CONCERNING THE HAIR OF MACROPROSOPUS

65. THIS is the tradition. From the skull of His head hang down a thousand thousand myriads; seven thousand and five hundred curling hairs, white and pure, like as wool when it is pure; which have not been mingled confusedly together lest inordinate disorder should be shown in his conformation; but all are in order, so that no one lock may go beyond another lock, nor one hair before another.

66. And in single curls are four hundred and ten locks of hair, according unto the number of the word *Qadosh*, Holy.[1]

67. But these hairs, all and singular, radiate into four hundred and ten worlds.

68. But these worlds alone are hidden and concealed, and no man knoweth them, save himself.

69. And he radiateth in seven hundred and twenty directions *(others say four hundred and twenty)*.

70. And in all the hairs is a fountain, which issueth from the hidden brain behind the wall of the skull.

71. And it shineth and goeth forth through that hair of Microprosopus, and from it is His brain formed; and thence that brain goeth forth into thirty and two paths.

72. And each curl radiateth and hangeth down arranged in beautiful form, and adorned with ornament, and they enshroud the skull.

73. But the curls of the hair are disposed on each side of the skull.

[1] For by Gematria Q + D + V + SH = 100 + 4 + 6 + 300 = 410.

74. Also we have said: Each hair is said to be the breaking of the hidden fountains, issuing from the concealed brain.

75. Also this is the tradition: From the hair of a man it is known what he is, whether rigorous or merciful, when he passeth over forty years; thus also when he is perfect in hair, in beard, and in the eyebrows of his eyes.

76. The curls of His hair hang down in order, and pure like unto *(pure)* wool, even unto his shoulders. Say we unto His shoulders? Nevertheless, even unto the rise of His shoulders, so that His neck may not be seen, because of that which is written, Jer. ii, 27: "Because they have turned away from Me the neck and not the face."

77. And the hair is less close to the ears, lest it should cover them; because it is written, Ps. cxxx, 2: "As Thine ears are open."

78. From hence His hair stretcheth out behind His ears. The whole is in equilibrium; one hair doth not go beyond another hair, *(they are)* in perfect disposition, and beautiful arrangement, and orderly condition.

79. It is the delight and joy of the just, who are in Microprosopus, to desire to behold and to conform unto that conformation which is in the Ancient One, the Most Concealed of all.

80. Thirteen curls of hair exist on the one side and on the other of the skull; *(they are)* about His face, and through them commenceth the division of the hair.

81. There is no left in that Ancient Concealed One, but all is right.[2]

82. He appeareth, and He appeareth not; He is concealed,

[2] Meaning there is no evil in Him, but all is good. So that, in the symbolic language of the Zohar, Macroprosopus is represented by a profile countenance, wherein one side is not seen, rather than by a full face, as in Microprosopus.

and He is not concealed; and that is in His conformation much more so than in Himself.

83. And concerning this the children of Israel wished to inquire in their heart, like as it is written, Exod. xvii, 7: "Is the Lord in the midst of us, or the Negatively Existent One?" *(Where they distinguished)* between Microprosopus, who is called Lord, and between Macroprosopus, who is called *Ain,* the Negatively Existent?

84. But why, then, were they punished? Because they did it not in love, but in temptation; like as it is written *(ibid.)*: "Because they tempted the Lord, saying, Is it the Lord in the midst of us, or is it the Negatively Existent One?"

85. In the parting of the hair proceedeth a certain path, which shineth into two hundred and seventy worlds, and from that *(again)* shineth a path wherein the just of the world to come shall shine.

86. That is what is written, Prov. iv, 18: "And the path of the just shall shine as the light, going forth, and shining more and more unto the perfect day."

87. And out of that is the path divided into six hundred and thirteen paths, which are distributed in Microprosopus.

88. As it is written concerning Him, Ps. xxv, 6: "All the paths of the Lord are mercy and truth," etc.

CHAPTER VIII

Concerning the Forehead of Macroprosopus

89. The forehead of His skull is the acceptation of acceptations, whereunto is opposed the acceptation of Microprosopus, like as it is written, Exod. xxviii, 38: "And it shall be upon His forehead alway for acceptation," etc.

90. And that forehead is called *Ratzon*, Willpower, because it is the ruler of the whole head and of the skull, which is covered by four hundred and twenty worlds.

91. And when it is uncovered, the prayers of the Israelites ascend.

92. "When is it uncovered?" Rabbi Schimeon was silent. He asked again a second time, "When?" Rabbi Schimeon said unto Rabbi Eleazar, his son, "When is it uncovered?"

93. He answered unto him: "In the time of the offering of the evening prayer on the Sabbath."

94. He said unto him: "For what reason?" He answered unto him: "Because at that time the lower judgment threateneth through Microprosopus; but that forehead is uncovered which is called 'Acceptation,' and then wrath is assuaged, and the prayer ascendeth.

95. "This is that which is written, Ps. lxix, 14: 'And I have prayed unto Thee, O Lord! in an acceptable time.'

96. "And the time of acceptance by the Ancient of Days[1] is here to be understood, and of the unveiling of the fore-

[1] Macroprosopus.

head; and because it is thus disposed at the offering of the evening prayer on the Sabbath."

97. Rabbi Schimeon spake unto Rabbi Eleazar, his son, and said: Blessed be thou, O my son! by the Ancient of Days; for thou hast found in that time in which thou hast need the acceptation of His forehead.

98. Come and behold! in these inferiors, when the forehead is uncovered, there is found fixed shamelessness.

99. This is the same which is written, Jer. iii, 3: "Yet thou hadst the forehead of a shameless woman, thou refusedst to be ashamed."

100. But when this forehead[2] is uncovered, inclination and acceptation are found in perfect form, and all wrath is quieted and subdued before Him.

101. From that forehead shine forth four hundred habitations of Judgments, when it is uncovered during that period of acceptation, and all things are at peace before it.

102. This is the same which is written, Dan. vii, 10: "The judgment was set"—that is, subsideth in its place, and the judgment is not exercised.

103. And this is the tradition: There is no hair found on that part, because it is opened and not covered.

104. It is covered, I say, and the executors of judgment behold this, and are pacified, and (judgment) is not exercised.

105. This is the tradition: This forehead hath been extended into two hundred and seventy thousand lights of the luminaries of the superior Eden.

106. This is the tradition: There existeth an Eden which shineth in Eden. The superior Eden, which is not uncovered, and is hidden in concealment, and is not distributed into the paths, like as it hath been said.

[2] That of Macroprosopus.

107. The inferior Eden is distributed into its paths; (*namely*) into thirty-two directions of its paths.

108. And although this Eden is distributed into its path, yet is it not known unto any, save unto Microprosopus.

109. But no man hath known the superior Eden, nor its paths, except Macroprosopus Himself.

110. Like as it is written, Job xxviii, 23: "God understandeth the way thereof, and He knoweth the place thereof."

111. "The Elohim understand the way thereof:" this is the inferior Eden, known unto Microprosopus. "And He hath known the place thereof:" this is the superior Eden, which the Ancient of Days hath known, the most abstruse of all.

CHAPTER IX

CONCERNING THE EYES OF MACROPROSOPUS

112. THE eyes of the White Head[1] are diverse from all other eyes. Above the eye is no eyelid, neither is there an eyebrow over it.

113. Wherefore? Because it is written, Ps. cxxi, 4: "Behold, He that keepeth Israel shall neither slumber nor sleep"; that is, the superior Israel.

114. Also it is written, Jer. xxxii, v, 19: "Whose eyes are open."

115. And this is the tradition. Seeing that all is operated through mercies, He hath not covering unto His eye, nor eyebrow above His eye; how little, then, doth the White Head require such.

116. Rabbi Schimeon spake unto Rabbi Abba, and said: "To what is this like?" He answered unto him: "To the whales and fishes of the sea, which have no coverings for their eyes, nor eyebrows above their eyes; who sleep not, and require not a protection for the eye.

117. "How much less doth the Ancient of the Ancient Ones require a protection, seeing that He far above His creatures watcheth over all things, and all things are nourished by Him, and He Himself sleepeth not.

118. "This is that which is written, Ps. cxxi, 4: 'Behold! He that keepeth Israel shall neither slumber nor sleep.' That is, the superior Israel.

---

[1] This, like Macroprosopus, is a title of Kether, the first Sephira.

119. "It is written Ps. xxxiii, 18: 'Behold the eye of the Lord is upon them that fear Him'; and it is written, Zech. iv, 10: 'They are the eyes of the Lord, running to and fro throughout the whole earth.'

120. "There is no contrariety *(between these sayings)*; one is concerning Microprosopus, and the other concerning Macroprosopus.

121. "And further, although there be two eyes, yet they are converted into one eye.

122. "This is pure in its whiteness, and so white that it includeth all whiteness.

123. "The first whiteness shineth, and ascendeth and descendeth for the purpose of combining with that which is connected *(with it)* in connection.

124. "This is the tradition: That whiteness darteth forth its rays, and igniteth three lights, which are called *Hod*, Glory, *Vehadar*, and Majesty, *Vachedoah*, and Joy; and they radiate in gladness and in perfection.

125. "The second whiteness shineth and ascendeth and descendeth, and darteth forth its rays, and igniteth three other lights, which are called *Netzach*,[2] Victory, *Chesed*, and Benignity, *Tiphereth*, and Beauty; and they radiate in perfection and in gladness.

126. "The third whiteness radiateth and shineth, and descendeth and ascendeth, and goeth forth from the part enclosing the brain, and darteth forth its rays toward the seventh middle light.

127. "And it formeth a path to the inferior brain, and formeth a path to the inferior, and all the inferior lights are thereby ignited."

---

[2] Netzach, Chesed, and Tiphereth, are respectively the seventh, fourth, and sixth Sephiroth.

128. Rabbi Schimeon said: Thou hast well spoken, and the Ancient of Days will open His eye upon thee in the time of thy necessity.

129. Another tradition runneth thus: Whiteness in whiteness, and whiteness which includeth all other whiteness.

130. The first whiteness shineth and ascendeth and descendeth in three lights on the left-hand side, and they radiate and are bathed in that whiteness, like as when a man batheth his body in good unguents and odors, in better than he at first possessed.

131. The second whiteness descendeth and ascendeth and shineth in three lights on the right-hand side, and they radiate and are bathed in that whiteness, like as when a man batheth in good unguents and odors, in better than he at first possessed.

132. The third whiteness shineth and ascendeth and descendeth, and goeth forth the light of the inner whiteness of the brain, and darteth forth its rays when necessary unto the black hair, and unto the head, and unto the brain of the head.

133. And it irradiateth the three crowns which remain, when it is needful, so that it may be uncovered, if that be pleasing unto the Most Ancient One hidden from all.

134. And this is the tradition: This eye is never closed; and there are two, and they are converted into one.

135. All is right; there is no left there. He sleepeth not and slumbereth not, and He requireth not protection. He is not such an one as hath need to defend Himself, for He defendeth all things, and He Himself waited upon all things, and in the sight of His eye are all things established.

136. This is the tradition: Where that eye closed even for one moment, no thing could subsist.

137. Therefore it is called the open eye, the holy eye, the

excellent eye, the eye of Providence, the eye which sleepeth not neither slumbereth, the eye which is the guardian of all things, the eye which is the subsistence of all things.

138. And concerning it is it written, Prov. xxii, 9, "The bountiful eye"; thou shalt not read "the blessed eye," but "it blesseth," for it is called "the bountiful eye," and by it are all things blessed.

139. And this is the tradition: There is no light in the inferior eye, so that it can be bathed in redness and blackness; except when it is beheld by that white brilliance of the superior eye which is called "the bountiful eye."

140. And to no man is it known when this superior holy eye may shine and may bathe the inferior; and when the just and the supernal blessed ones are about to be beheld in that Wisdom.

141. This is that which is written, Isa. lii, 8: "For they shall see eye to eye"; When? "When the Lord shall bring again Zion." Also, it is written, Num. xiv, 14: "That Thou, the Lord, art seen eye to eye."

142. And unless the bountiful superior eye were to look down upon and bathe the inferior eye, the universe could not exist even a single moment.

143. This is the tradition in the "Book of Concealed Mystery"; Providence ariseth from the inferior eye when the highest splendor shineth down upon it, and that highest splendor goeth forth into the inferior; for from it are all things illuminated.

144. This is that which is written, Num. xiv, 14: "That Thou, O the Lord! art seen eye to eye." Also it is written, Ps. xxxiii, 18: "Behold the eye of the Lord is upon them that fear Him." And it is written, Zech. iv, 10: "The eyes of the Lord running to and fro throughout the whole earth."

145. "The eye of the Lord is upon them that fear Him," if they be upright. This is the superior eye. On the contrary,

when it is said, "The eyes of the Lord run to and fro," this is the eye which is below.

146. This is the tradition: On what account was Joseph worthy, so that the evil eye had no dominion over him? Because that he was worthy of being beheld by the superior benign eye.

147. This is what is written, Gen. xlix, 22: "Joseph is the son of a fruitful bough; the son of a fruitful bough above Ayin." Why "the son of a fruitful bough above Ayin"?[3] As though to imply, "because of that eye which beheld him."

148. Also it is written, Prov. xxii, 9: "The bountiful eye shall be blessed." Why? Because it giveth its bread unto the poor.

149. Why is it said in the singular number? Come and see. In the eyes which are inferior are a right eye and a left eye, and they are of two diverse colors.

150. But in this instance there is no left eye, and they both ascend in one path, and all are right. And on that account is one eye mentioned, and not two.

151. And this is the tradition: This eye, which is the eye of observation, is ever open, ever smiling, ever glad.

152. Such are not the inferiors, who in themselves have redness, and blackness, and whiteness—three colors; and are not always open, for there are eyelids as a protection over these eyes.

153. And concerning this matter it is written, Ps. xliv, 23: "Awake, O Lord: why sleepest Thou?" And, 2 Kings xix, 16: "Open Thine eyes, O Lord."

154. When they are opened, for some are they opened for good, and on some are they opened for evil.

155. Woe unto him upon whom it is opened, so that the eye is mingled with redness, and unto whom the redness

---

[3] The word Ayin means eye.—TRANS.

appeareth, spreading across that eye. Who can escape from it?

156. But the Ancient of Days is blessed, presiding over that eye the white brilliance of whiteness, seeing that also it is of such whiteness that it endureth all whiteness.

157. Blessed also is his portion whom that brilliance of all whiteness irradiateth.

158. And concerning this certainly it is written, Prov. xxii, 9: "The good eye is to be blessed." And it is written, Isa. ii, 5: "Be ye present, O house of Jacob, and let us walk in the light of the Lord!"

159. This is the tradition: Save in all these instances, the name of the Ancient One is concealed from all, and is not mentioned in the law, save in one place, where Micropro-sopus sware unto Abraham.

160. Like as it is written, Gen. xxii, 16: "By Myself have I sworn, saith the Lord." (*Understand*) that this is said concerning Microprosopus.

161. Also it is written, Gen. xlviii, 20: "In thee shall Israel bless." That is, the superior Israel.

162. Also it is written, Isa. xlix, 3: "Israel, in whom I will be glorified." In these passages the Ancient of Days is called Israel.

163. But we have also stated that the Ancient of Days is called by His name, yet both this (*statement*) and the other are correct.

164. This is the tradition: It is written, Dan. vii, 9: "I beheld until the thrones were cast down, and the Ancient of Days did sit."

165. "The thrones were cast down." What is this? He spake unto Rabbi Yehuda, and said: "Stand in thy place and explain these thrones."

166. Rabbi Yehuda answered: "It is written (*ibid.*) 'His

throne is of fiery flame'; and upon that throne sat the Ancient of Days.

167. "For what reason? Because thus is the tradition: If the Ancient of Days were not seated upon that throne, the universe could no longer exist before that throne.

168. "When the Ancient of Days sitteth upon that throne, it is subject unto Him. For He who sitteth upon it ruleth over it.

169. "But at that time when He departeth from that throne, and sitteth upon another throne, the first throne is overturned, lest any should rule over it save the Ancient One, who alone can sit upon it."

170. Rabbi Schimeon spake unto Rabbi Yehuda, and said: "May thy way be ordained for thee, and may it be pointed out (unto thee) by the Ancient of Days!"

CHAPTER X

171. AND come, behold, lo! it is written, Isaiah xli, 4: "I the Lord, (*am*) first and with the last. I am HE HIMSELF" (*Hoa*).

172. All things are *Hoa*, He Himself, and He Himself is hidden on every side. So also is His nose.

173. From the nose is the face known.

174. And come—see! What is the (*difference*) between the Ancient One and Microprosopus? Over these nostrils He ruleth; one of which is life, and the other is the life of life.

175. This nose is as a mighty gallery, whence His spirit rusheth forth upon Microprosopus, and they call it the Giver.

176. And it is thus: The Spirit descendeth; and again the Spirit from hence proceedeth through those nostrils.

177. One is the Spirit; She goeth forth unto Microprosopus, so that he may be aroused in the Garden of Eden.

178. And one is She the Spirit of Life, through Whom in process of time the sons of David hope to know Wisdom.

179. And from that gallery ariseth the Spirit, and proceedeth from the concealed brain, and at length resteth upon King Messiach.

180. Like as it is written, Isaiah xi, 2: "And the Spirit of the Lord shall rest upon him, the Spirit of Wisdom and Understanding, the Spirit of Counsel and Might, the Spirit of Knowledge, and of the Fear of the Lord."

181. Apparently four spirits (*are described*) here. But we

have already said that the Spirit is one; why, then, are three (*others added unto it?*). Arise, Rabbi Yosi, in thy place.

182. Rabbi Yosi arose and said: "In the days of King Messiach, one shall not say unto the other, 'Teach me this Wisdom.'

183. "Because it is thus written, Jer. xxxi, 34: 'A man shall no more teach his neighbor, etc., because all shall know Me, from the least of them even unto the greatest of them.'

184. "And in that time shall the Ancient of Days arouse His Spirit which proceedeth from His brain, the most concealed of all.

185. "And when that cometh forth all the inferior spirits are aroused with Her.

186. "And who are they? They are the holy crowns of Microprosopus.

187. "And there are six other spirits which are given. They are those of whom it is written: 'The Spirit of Wisdom and Intelligence, the Spirit of Counsel and Might, the Spirit of Knowledge and of the Fear of the Lord.'

188. "For thus is the tradition: It is written, 1 Kings ii, 12: 'And Solomon sat upon the throne of David.' Also it is written, 1 Kings x, 19: 'The throne had six steps.'

189. "And King Messiach will be seated on those seven (steps). These are those six, and the Spirit of the Ancient of Days, Who is above them, is the seventh.

190. "Like as it is said, 'There are three spirits which comprehend three others.' "

191. Rabbi Schimeon said unto him: "Thy spirit shall rest in the world to come."

192. Come—behold! It is written, Ezek. xxxvii, 9: "Thus saith the Lord, 'Come from the four winds, O Spirit!' " But what have the four winds of the world to do with this?

193. Nevertheless, the four winds are aroused; those

three, namely, and the Spirit of the Concealed Ancient One; whence there are four.

194. And thus is the matter; because when that one is produced, three others are produced with it, who in themselves comprehend three others.

195. But it is the will of that Holy and Blessed One to produce the one Spirit, Who in Herself includeth all others.

196. Because it is written, Ezek. xxxvii, 9: "From the four spirits, come, O spirit!" It is not written thus: "Ye four spirits, come!" but "From the four spirits, come!"

197. And in the days of King Messiach there shall be no need that one should teach another; for that one Spirit Who in Herself includeth all spirits, knoweth all Wisdom and Understanding, Counsel and Might, (*and is*) the Spirit of Science and of the Fear of the Lord; because She is the Spirit comprehending all spirits.

198. Therefore is it written, "From the four spirits"; which are those four comprehended in the seven steps of which we have just spoken, § 189.

199. And this is the tradition: All things are comprehended in this Spirit of the Ancient of the Ancient Ones,[1] Who proceedeth from the concealed brain, into the gallery of the nostrils.

200. And come—see! Wherein is the difference between the nose (*of Macroprosopus*), and the nose (*of Microprosopus*).

201. The nose of the Ancient of Days is life in every part. Concerning the nose of Microprosopus it is written, Ps. xviii, 8: "There went up smoke out of His nostrils, and fire out of His mouth devoured," etc.

202. There goeth up a smoke through His nostrils, and out of that smoke is a fire kindled.

203. When that smoke goeth up, what afterward fol-

---

[1] *I.e.,* The Spirit.

loweth? Coals are kindled by it. What is the meaning of this "by it"? By that smoke, out of that nose, out of that fire.

204. This is the tradition: When Rav Hammenuna the elder wished to offer up his prayer, he said, "I pray unto the Lord of the nostrils, unto the Lord of the nostrils do I pray."

205. And this is that which is written, Isa. xlviii, 9: "In my praise (that is, My nose) will I refrain My nostrils for thee." In which place the sentence is concerning the Ancient of Days.

206. This is the tradition. The size of this nose is so vast that three hundred and seventy-five worlds are supported by it, which all adhere unto Microprosopus.

207. This is the praise of the conformation of the nose.

208. And this, and all forms of the Ancient of Days, are seen, and are not seen; they are seen by the lords of lords—viz., by pious men—and they are not seen by any others.

CHAPTER XI

CONCERNING THE BEARD OF MACROPROSOPUS IN GENERAL

209. RABBI SCHIMEON began, and said: Woe unto him who extendeth his hand unto that most glorious supernal beard of the Holy Ancient One, the concealed of all.

210. This is the praise of that beard; the beard which is concealed and most precious in all its dispositions; the beard which neither the superiors nor the inferiors have known;[1] the beard which is the praise of all praise; the beard to which neither man, nor prophet, nor saint hath approached so as to behold it.

211. The beard, whose hairs hang down even unto the breast, white as snow; the adornment of adornments, the concealment of concealments, the truth of all truths.

212. It is said in the "Book of Concealed Mystery": That beard, the truth of all (*truths*), proceedeth from the place of the ears, and descendeth around the mouth of the Holy One; and descendeth and ascendeth, covering (*the cheeks which it calleth*) the places of copious fragrance; (*it is*) white with ornament: and it descendeth in the equilibrium (*of balanced power*), and furnisheth a covering unto the midst of the breast.

213. That is the beard of adornment, true and perfect, from which flow down thirteen fountains, scattering the most precious balm of splendor.

[1] Because it is the beard of Macroprosopus, the Concealed Ancient One.

214. This is disposed in thirteen forms.

215. In the first disposition are classed the hairs from above, and it commenceth from that portion of the hair of His head which is above His ears; and descendeth in one tress before the apertures of the ears in the most perfect equilibrium, even unto the corner of the mouth.

216. In the second disposition are classed the hairs from the corner of the mouth, and they ascend even unto the other corner of the mouth in perfectly equated order.

217. The third disposition is from midway between the nostrils; beneath those two apertures there goeth forth a certain path, and the hair is wanting in that path; but on either side of and bordering that path it is fuller and in perfect order.

218. The hairs which are classed under the fourth disposition descend below the mouth from the one corner even unto the other corner, in perfect order.

219. The fifth disposition. Beneath the mouth proceedeth another path, from the region of the superior path, and those two paths are impressed on His mouth on this side and on that.

220. The hairs which are classed in the sixth disposition ascend and come from beneath upward unto the corner of the mouth, and cover the places of copious fragrance, even unto the upper corner of the mouth, and the hair descendeth at the corner of the opening, and across below the mouth.

221. In the seventh disposition the hair terminateth, and there are seen two apples in the places of copious fragrance, beautiful and joyful in aspect, because (*in that aspect*) is the universe maintained. And this is that which is said, Prov. xvi, 16: "In the light of the king's countenance is life."

222. In the eighth disposition a certain tress of hair proceedeth round about the beard, and (*the hairs*) hang down equilibrated even unto the chest.

223. In the ninth disposition the hairs of the beard are interwoven and mingled with those hairs which hang in equilibrium; which hang even thus, so that none is pre-eminent over another.

224. In the tenth disposition the hairs descend beneath the beard, and cover the throat beneath the beard.

225. The eleventh disposition is, that no hairs are pre-eminent over other hairs, and they are restored into perfect proportion.

226. The twelfth disposition is that the hairs do not hang over the mouth, and that the mouth is uncovered in every part, and that the hair surrounding it is beautiful.

227. The thirteenth disposition is that the hairs hang down on this side and on that beneath the beard, furnishing a covering in beautiful adornment, even unto the chest.

228. Nothing is seen of the whole countenance and of the places of fragrance, except those beautiful white apples which produce the life of the universe; and they radiate gladness upon Microprosopus.

229. Through those thirteen dispositions do they flow down, and the thirteen fountains of precious oil issue forth, and they flow down through all those inferiors, and in that oil do they shine, and with that oil are they anointed.

230. The beard of ornament of the Ancient of the Ancient Ones, the most concealed of all things, is configurated in thirteen dispositions.

231. From the two beautiful apples[2] of His countenance is the face of Macroprosopus illuminated; and whatsoever is white and rosy is found below;[3] it shineth and radiateth from that light.

---

[2] The cheeks.

[3] That is, the lower Sephiroth reflect and partake of the properties of the superior emanations.

232. Those thirteen dispositions are found in the beard. And in proportion to the purity of his beard,[4] according to its dispositions, is a man said to be true; for also whosoever (*in sleep*) beholdeth his beard, that man is very desirous of truth.

233. We have taught in the "Book of Concealed Mystery," that certain (*dispositions*) are found in the universe, according to those thirteen (*dispositions*) which depend from that venerable beard, and they are opened out into the thirteen gates of mercies.

234. And he who extendeth his hand in swearing, also doth the same if he swear by the thirteen[5] dispositions of the beard: these are in Arikh Anpin, or Macroprosopus.

235. In Zauir Anpin, or Microprosopus, how many are there? He said unto Rabbi Isaac: "Arise in thy place, and describe the beard of the Holy King according unto the arrangements of its parts. How are these arranged?"

236. Rabbi Isaac arose; he commenced and said, Micah vii, 18: "What god is like unto Thee," etc.; "Thou shalt give truth unto Jacob," etc.

237. "We have learned by tradition that herein are thirteen sections seen, and they all proceed from the thirteen fountains of excellent oil, of the parts of the holy beard of the Ancient of the Ancient Ones.

238. "Tradition: A most secret thing is this disposition of the beard. Secret is it and hidden; hidden, yet not hidden; concealed, yet not concealed in its dispositions; known, yet unknown.

[4] By the beard is of course symbolically meant the atmosphere of good or bad deeds with which a man surrounds himself during his life. Concerning dreaming of the beard, see the "Book of Concealed Mystery," ch. iii. § § 17, 18.

[5] Thirteen is by Gematria the number of *Achad,* Unity. For A + CH + D = 1 + 8 + 4 = 13.

239. "The first disposition. We have learned that the single locks and the single hairs do not mutually adhere unto each other; and that the hairs of the beard take their rise from the disposition of the hair (of the head).

240. "This matter is worthy of examination. If all the hairs of the head and the hairs of the venerable supernal beard are balanced in one equilibrium, wherefore are some long, and others not so long?

241. "Wherefore are not the hairs of the beard constant in the same proportion of length? These also are firm; while those which are on the head are not firm, but soft.

242. "Therefore is it said that (in Macroprosopus) all the hairs descend equally from the head and beard; for the hair of the head is prolonged even unto the shoulders, so that it may reach unto the head of Microprosopus, from that flux of the one brain unto the other.

243. "And because they are not firm (also it is necessary that they be soft).[6]

244. "We have learned by tradition. What is that which is written, Prov. i, 20: 'Wisdom (*plural in Hebrew, CHKMVTH, not CHKMH*) will cry without'; and at the end of the verse it is written, 'She (*singular*) will utter Her voice in the streets.' In this text the beginning doth neither agree with the end, nor the end with the beginning.

245. "Therefore is it said: Wisdom will cry without when She passeth from the concealed brain of Macroprosopus unto the brain of Microprosopus, through those longer hairs; and thus as it were extrinsically those two brains are connected and become in this way one brain.

246. "Since there is not subsistence in the inferior brain except by the preservation of the supernal brain.

---

[6] *I.e.*, If they be not the one, they must be the other.

247. "And when this proflux is instituted from the one, namely, into the other, this hath place which is written, 'She will utter Her voice'; namely, in the singular number.

248. "And because She passeth over from brain unto brain through those long hairs, the same (hairs) are not found to be firm.

249. "Wherefore? Because if they were firm, Wisdom could not be conducted by them unto the brain.

250. "Because Wisdom cometh not from man, who is stern and wrathful, like as it is written, Eccles. ix, 17: 'The words of wise men are heard in quiet.'

251. "And thence we learn that in him whose hair is firm, wisdom dwelleth not.[7]

252. "But because these are long (the others are soft) in order that they may bring assistance to all.

253. "How, unto all? So that it may have entrance into the marrow of the spine of the back, which is connected with the brain.

254. "And because the hair of the head doth not hang over the hairs of the beard, since the hair of the head hangeth down, and is drawn back behind the ears, and doth not overhang the beard; because it is not necessary to mingle these with those, but all are separated in their own paths.

255. "We have learned by tradition. All the hairs, as well of the head as of the beard, are white as snow.

256. "And we have learned. Those which are in the beard are all firm. Wherefore? Because those are firm accordingly, that they may firmly mark out their thirteen measurements from the Ancient of the Ancient Ones.[8]

---

[7] I.e., Meaning symbolically, "in him who is hardened."

[8] I have before remarked that this refers to the unity of the Deity: *Achad*, One; which by Gematria yields 13.

257. "And those measurements take their beginning from before the ears.

258. "And those measurements have been included within certain limitations, in order that they should not be confounded with each other. (Others read the passage thus: Because they are communicated unto the inferiors. For this have we been taught. The hairs commence before the ears, because they have been separated, and are not to be mingled with the others," etc.)

259. "But if thou sayest that other (sacred passages) are not given, analogous to these (measurements), thou art in error. For thus is the tradition: "The thirteen measurements of the mercies of the Most Holy Ancient One (are symbolized by these clauses of) Mic. vii, 18: 'What God is like unto Thee?' the first.

260. " 'Pardoning iniquity'; the second.

261. " 'And passeth by the transgression'; the third.

262. " 'Of the remnant of His heritage'; the fourth.

263. " 'He retaineth not His anger for ever'; the fifth.

264. " 'Because He delighteth in mercy'; the sixth.

265. " 'Again, He will have compassion on us'; the seventh.

266. " 'He will subdue our iniquities'; the eighth.

267. " 'And Thou wilt cast all their iniquities into the depths of the sea'; the ninth.

268. " 'Thou wilt give truth unto Jacob'; the tenth.

269. " 'Mercy unto Abraham'; the eleventh.

270. " 'Which Thou hast sworn unto our fathers'; the twelfth.

271. " 'From the days of old'; the thirteenth.

272. " 'Unto these correspond in the law,' Exod. xxxiv, 6: 'God merciful and gracious,' etc. And those are the Inferiors.

273. "And if thou sayest, 'Why did not Moses pronounce

those majestic words?'[9] it shall be answered unto thee: 'Moses hath no duty to perform save in the place where judgment is found; and in the place where judgment is found it is not necessary to speak thus.'[10]

274. "And Moses spake not, save in that time when the Israelites had sinned and judgment was impending; hence Moses spake only in that place wherein judgment is found.

275. "But in another place the prophet hath instituted the order of the praise of the Ancient of Days.[11]

276. "And those thirteen forms of the supreme holy beard, concealed with many concealments, are most powerful to subdue and mitigate all the stern decrees of the judgments.

277. "What man is he who looketh back upon that most secret, holy supernal beard, who is not confounded before it?

278. "Because also all the hairs are hard and firm in their disposition.

279. "But if thou sayest, 'What if they be so? Surely the lower hairs are black: why are these not as those?'

280. "Nevertheless, thus is the tradition: It is written, Cant. v, 11: 'His locks are bushy and black as a raven.'

281. "Also it is written, Dan. vii, 18: 'The hair of His head like pure wool.'

282. "There is no contradiction here, for the one is said of the supernal beard, but the other of the inferior beard.[12]

---

[9] Apparently meaning that, as the words of the text denote, it was the Lord and not Moses that proclaimed the titles of the Lord aloud.

[10] *I.e.*, mentioning the merciful characteristics of the Deity, who is represented as the equilibrium of justice and mercy.

[11] That is, of AHIH, as distinct from IHVH.

[12] The hair and beard of Macroprosopus, as distinct from that of Microprosopus. (See the "Book of Concealed Mystery," ch. iii. § 16.)

283. "Also because when the law was given forth unto the Israelites, it was written in black fire upon white fire.

284. "Also the foundation of the matter cometh from those hairs; because they are found (arising) out of the (supernal) brain, and stretching down unto the inferior brain.

285. "Also because these are above the beard. Hence the beard is distinct, and all its forms are found separated (each from the other); so that the beard is alone, and its hairs are also distinct."

CHAPTER XII

CONCERNING THE BEARD OF MACROPROSOPUS
IN PARTICULAR; AND, IN THE FIRST PLACE,
CONCERNING ITS FIRST PART

286. "THE first disposition is that which commenceth almost at the beginning of the hair.

287. "Also we have learned: No beard (*i.e.*, no part of this beard) is found which doth not (virtually) arise from the brain of the head (or from the heart).[1]

288. "But in this (last section) this (first part of the beard) is not considered as distinct (from the others). For in this chapter only this first form (*or portion of the beard*) is to be considered, which descendeth from the beginning of the hair, and it hath this peculiarity (*namely, that it riseth directly from the brain, which cannot altogether be said concerning the other parts of the beard*).

289. "And this is to be kept perfectly distinct from this beard—namely, that which exists from the head (formed into), one thousand worlds, sealed with a most pure seal, with a seal which includeth all seals.

290. "The length of that portion of hair descending before the ears is not equal to the length (of the beard itself); neither doth it twine together, nor hang down far.

291. "But those hairs, when they flow down, are extended, and depend.

292. "And the beginning of the first disposition consists

[1] The heart being considered as the central motor of the body.

of thirty and one equal locks, extended even unto the beginning of the mouth.

293. "Also three hundred and ninety hairs are found in each lock.

294. "Those thirty and one equal locks, which exist in the first disposition (of the beard) are strong, in order that they may dispose the inferiors according to the number of *El*.[2]

295. "What is this *El?* Mighty and Powerful One.

296. "And among those single locks are distributed one and thirty dominating worlds, so that they may be extended[3] (correctly) neither on this side nor on that.

297. "And out of each one of these worlds a partition is made into a thousand worlds of desires and of great pleasures.

298. "And they are all concealed in the commencement of the beard, which representeth strength; and they are included in that (name) AL.

299. "And notwithstanding is AL Himself disposed toward mercies, because in Him the Ancient of Days is mitigated and included and extended.

300. "Wherefore even unto the mouth? Because it is written, Dan. vii, 9: 'The judgment was set, and the books were opened.'

301. "What is this? 'And the judgment was set.' It was set in that place, so that it might not have dominion.

302. "This is that which is written, Isa. ix, 15: 'Wonderful, Counsellor, God the Mighty One.' That is, *El,* such a one who also is mighty, but is rendered mild through the holy beard of the Ancient of Days.

---

[2] *El,* God, the Mighty One, is equivalent by Gematria to the number 31; for A + L = 1 + 30 = 31.

[3] For were they extended, the number would be altered, and it would consequently no longer = AL.

303. "And an Arcanum is concealed in that place wherein it is written, Mic. vii, 18: 'What *El*, like unto Thee?' Because of the Ancient of Days it is spoken in the form of the configuration of the holy supernal beard.

304. "The first world, which proceedeth from the first disposition, hath dominion over, and descendeth and ascendeth in a thousand times a thousand myriads of myriads of shield-bearers, and by it are they comprehended under a great seal.

305. "The second world, which proceedeth from that disposition, hath dominion over and descendeth and ascendeth in fifty-seven thousand bodyguards, who are the lords of lamentations; and these are connected with it for the purpose of disposing the neck of the spine.[4]

306. "The third world, which goeth forth from that arrangement, hath dominion over and descendeth and ascendeth in sixty-nine thousand authors of grief, who are upheld by it, like as metal (is upheld) by the tongs (of the smith).

307. "And by that conformation all those are subjected, and mitigated in the bitterness of tears, which become sweet in the great sea.[5]

308. "Who is he who beholdeth this conformation of the holy beard, excellent and venerable, who is not overcome with shame thereby?

309. "Who can comprehend the mystery of those locks of hair which hang down from Him, the Ancient One?

310. "He is set on the crown of crowns, which are the crowns of all crowns, and the crowns which are not com-

---

[4] This is of course simply pursuing the symbolism involved in the idea of Macroprosopus, being typified by a vast countenance or head.

[5] By the great sea, Binah, the third Sephira, is probably meant. (See the "Book of Concealed Mystery," ch. i. § 28).

prehended in the other crowns; I say, of those crowns which are not as the other crowns, for the inferior crowns are comprehended by them.[6]

311. "And therefore are those forms (arranged in) such conformations, whereunto the inferior forms adhere; and they are the dispositions in which He[7] is disposed Who hath need that He may be blessed by Him,[8] and Who desireth blessing.

312. "For whensoever the dispositions take the form of these, blessings are found beneath them; and It Is that which It Is.[9]

313. "All things are comprehended in those dispositions; all things raise themselves up in order that they may receive these dispositions of the Mighty King, of the Ancient One, the most concealed of all. And all those are mitigated by those ordinations of the King, the Ancient One.

314. "We have learned: Unless the Ancient of the Ancient Ones, the Holy of the Holy Ones, were disposed in those conformations, neither the superiors nor the inferiors would be found, and all things would be as though they existed not.

315. "Also we have learned by tradition: how far do those conformations of the beard radiate splendor? Even

[6] The Sephiroth are symbolized by crowns. In this sense the "crown of crowns" is Kether, the first Sephira, the Ancient One; the crowns of all crowns will be the first three Sephiroth; and the inferiors will be the lower Sephiroth, and those other forms which are dependent on them, symbolized by the crowns of the twenty-four elders in the Apocalypse, which latter is a purely qabalistical work, and is unintelligible without the qabalistical keys.

[7] Microprosopus.

[8] Macroprosopus.

[9] Cf. Exodus iii, 14.

unto the thirteen inferiors; and whensoever those thirteen are found, those shine.[10]

316. "And all of them are found in the number thirteen.

317. "Therefore is the beard of the King, the Ancient One, most venerable among all, at once in its entirety concealed, and most excellent.

318. "And because it is most excellent before all things, and concealed, there is no mention made concerning it in any place in the law, and it is not manifested.

319. "But what beard is manifested? The beard of the Great High Priest, and from that beard descendeth the influx unto the inferior beard of the inferior high priest.[11]

320. "How is the beard of the high priest disposed? The beard of the high priest is disposed in eight conformations. Because also the high priest hath eight vestments, when the ointment descendeth upon his beard.

321. "This is that which is written, Ps. cxxxiii, 2: 'Like the precious oil upon the head descending upon the beard, the beard of Aaron, which descendeth according to the proportion of his attributes,' etc.

322. "And whence is this to us? Because it is written in the same place: 'Also for brethren to dwell together in equality.' The word 'also' increaseth the signification of the inferior high priest.

323. "Seeing that in the same way as the inferior high priest ministereth in the high priesthood, so also, if it be

[10] This section refers to the statement that Macroprosopus pours forth His splendor upon Microprosopus, so that the latter shines by reflected light.

[11] The Great High Priest is the son, Microprosopus, symbolized on earth by the High Priest. Compare what St. Paul says about Christ being our Great High Priest.

permitted to say so, doth the High Priest above minister in His high priesthood.

324. "This is the first ordination of the beard of the Ancient One, the most concealed of all."

325. Rabbi Schimeon said unto him: "It is justly thy due, Rabbi Isaac, that thou shouldest be under the ornament of the conformation of the beard, and that thou shouldest receive the light of the countenance of the Ancient of Days, the Ancient of the Ancient Ones. Blessed is thy portion, and blessed be my lot with thee in the world to come."

CHAPTER XIII

Concerning the Second Part of the Beard of Macroprosopus

326. "Arise, Rabbi Chisqiah, and stand in thy place, and declare the worthiness of this part of the holy beard."

327. Rabbi Chisqiah arose, and began his speech and said, Cant. vii, 10: "I am my beloved's, and his desire is toward me.

328. "Who is under consideration here, that 'I am my beloved's'? and because that 'his desire is toward me'?

329. "I have meditated, and lo! I have beheld the most excellent light of the supernal lights.

330. "It shone forth, and ascended on three hundred and twenty-five sides.

331. "And in that light was a certain obscurity washed away, like as when a man batheth in a deep river, whose divided waters flow round him on every side from that part which is above.

332. "And that light ascendeth unto the shore of the deep superior sea,[1] for all good openings and dignities are disclosed in that opening.

333. "I asked of them what might be the interpretation of that which I beheld; and, commencing they replied, 'Nosha Auan, Thou hast beheld iniquity being taken away.' "

334. He said: "This is the second disposition," and sat down.

---

[1] Binah, the third Sephira, which is called the "sea" in the "Book of Concealed Mystery." It answers to the first letter H, *He*, in the Lord.

335. Rabbi Schimeon said: Now is the universe united together (or mitigated). Blessed be thou, Rabbi Chisqiah, of the Ancient of the Ancient Ones!

336. Rabbi Schimeon said: All the lights are congregated together which come under this holy seal.

337. I bear witness that the highest heavens from the highest (powers) are above me, and the highest holy earth from the supernals, because now I can see what man hath not beheld from that time, when Moses for the second time ascended the mountain of Sinai.

338. For I see that my countenance shineth like the vehement splendor of the sun, who is about to issue forth for the healing of the universe.[2]

339. Like as it is written, Mal. iv, 2: "But unto you that fear my name shall the sun of righteousness arise, and healing in his wings."

340. Furthermore, I know that my countenance shineth; Moses neither knew nor perceived (the fact).

341. Like as it is written, Exod. xxxiv, 29: "And Moses knew not that the skin of his face shone."

342. Furthermore, I behold before me with mine eyes those thirteen sculptured (forms of the beard of Macroprosopus), and like flaming light did they shine.

343. And when the second of those (dispositions) was explained by thy mouth, that same at once was raised, and conformed, and crowned, and concealed in the concealment of the forms of the beard, but all the others were reinstated (in outward form).[3]

344. And what is more, that one (formation), whilst it was

[2] This phrase "splendor of the sun, who is" etc., evidently refers to the sixth Sephira, Tiphereth, or beauty, the splendor of the countenance of Microprosopus, while the "universe" refers to Malkuth.

[3] While Rabbi Chisqiah was speaking Rabbi Schimeon had this vision of the conformations of the beard.

explained by thy mouth, flamed forth in splendor, and was crowned with a crown, and seated upon a throne, like a king in the midst of his army.

345. And when the explanation ceased it ascended, and was crowned with a holy crown, and ordained, and concealed, and again placed among the forms of the holy beard; and thus with (the forms) all and singular.

346. Be ye glad, O my holy companions! for surely *(the universe)* shall not be in such a condition until King Messiach shall come.

CHAPTER XIV

CONCERNING THE THIRD PART OF THE BEARD
OF MACROPROSOPUS

347. "ARISE, Rabbi Chisqiah, for the second time."

348. We have learned that before Rabbi Chisqiah arose, a voice came forth and said: "One angel doth not undertake two messages."

349. Rabbi Schimeon was disturbed, and said: "Assuredly, let each (*of you*) speak singly in his place (*in respect of the symbolism of the seven inferiors*); but as for myself, and Rabbi Eleazar my son, and Rabbi Abba, we (*three*) refer unto the highest and complete perfection (*of the whole decad*). Arise, Rabbi Chiya."[1]

350. Rabbi Chiya arose, and, commencing said, Jer. i, 6:

---

[1] On a little consideration it will be seen that this meeting of ten of the principal Rabbis—*viz.,* Schimeon, Eleazar, Abba, Yehuda, Yosi Ben Jacob, Isaac, Chisqiah Ben Rav, Chiya, Yosi, and Yisa—was intended to be symbolical of the ten Sephiroth, wherein, furthermore, the three first-named were also representative of the great trinity of the crown, the king, and the queen. In other words, to speak plainly, the whole arrangement of this assembly was closely similar to the constitution of a masonic lodge. Confer also § 13 of this book, wherein these three Rabbis further symbolize the "Three Pillars" of the Sephiroth—this assembly of the ten forms of the Greater Holy Assembly. But on reference to the "Idra Zuta" we shall find that the Lesser Assembly consists of only seven Rabbis, of which the seventh, Rabbi Isaac, came in later than the others. These seven were Schimeon, Eleazar, Abba, Yehuda, Yosi Ben Jacob, Chiya, and Isaac. (Conf. "Idra Zuta," § 13.)

"Ahah Adonai the Lord! [2] 'Ah, Lord the Lord! behold, I cannot speak, for I am a child.'

351. "Therefore, why was it that Jeremiah could not speak, seeing that many sayings had passed from his lips prior to his saying this? Did he not therefore lie (*when he said*) that which is written (*in the text*): 'Behold, I cannot *Deber,* speak'?

352. "But we have learned that God influenced him so that he should speak to this end. For this is the tradition: "What is the difference between *Debur,* and *Amirah?* 'Amirah' is, as it were (*simple*) speech, wherein is required no especial uplifting of the voice; 'Debur' is public speaking, wherein is indeed necessary (*considerable*) elevation of voice and (*loud*) proclamation of words.'

353. "Since it is written, Exod. xx, 1: 'And God spake all these words, saying.'

354. "And according to what we have learned (*by tradition*), 'The whole earth heard this *Debur,* speech, and the whole earth trembled.' Because also it is written: '*Vayedeber,* and He spoke forth.' And it is not written: '*Vayomar,* and He said.'

355. "So also in this place: 'Behold! I cannot speak, *Deber';* that is, as a herald, by declaring an address, and convincing the world through the Holy Spirit.

356. "If thus be the matter, this is also to be noted which is written: '*Vayedeber the Lord;* and the Lord spake forth unto Moses, saying.' Nevertheless, what one of the prophets was so great as Moses? For never was any man so worthy as he; for he heard the *Debur,* loud voice, like the proclamation of a herald, and he feared not, neither did he tremble; while

[2] This is the Hebrew text of the Polyglot Bible, but in that of the "Idra Rabba," *"Ahah the Lord Elohim,"* is substituted for *"Adonai the Lord."*

the other prophets trembled even at *Amirah*, the speech, and were greatly afraid.

357. "Also we have learned that through the first and second dispositions of the beard it is necessary to pass on to the third; like as it is written, Job xxxiii, 29: 'Behold, God worketh all this with man by three paths.'[3]

358. "And come, behold! it is necessary through the two first conformations that thou pass on unto the third, because the third form is in the midst.

359. "For, under the nose,[4] beneath the two nostrils, there issueth a certain path, and from that path the hairs are wanting.

360. "Wherefore are they wanting? Because it is written, Mic. vii, 18: '*Va-Ghober Ghal Peshang*, and passing over transgression.' Therefore is that path prepared (*namely*) for the purpose of passing over (*transgression*).

361. "And therefore that path resideth beneath the nostrils of the nose; and the hairs do not grow in that path, because it subdueth iniquities.

362. "For it is written: 'Passing over transgression,' for the purpose of passing over unto the sacred mouth, in order that it may say, 'I HAVE PARDONED.'

363. "We have learned that many threatened vials of wrath look for this mouth, and to none among them is it manifested; for it is withdrawn and guarded around; it is known, and it is not known.

364. "We have learned in the 'Book of Concealed Mystery': What is this which is written (*in this disposition of the letters in this*) word, *Peshang?* If they be first, the word

---

[3] The same word which is here rendered thus is translated in the ordinary version of the Bible, "oftentimes."

[4] See § 217 of this book, and also the "Book of Concealed Mystery," ch. ii. § 8.

'Ghober, passing over,' hath place; if, on the other hand, not so, the word *'Peshang,* transgression,' hath place.

365. "What doth this phrase teach, 'passing over transgression'? *Shephau,* influence, (*it teacheth*) if SH (*in PSHO*) be placed before the P.[5]

366. "If they are not just, it remaineth (*i.e., the influence*), and passeth not over into Microprosopus.

367. "What is the difference between the one and the other? In Microprosopus (*the matter standeth thus*): this path descendeth beneath the nostrils of His nose. It is written, Num. xii, 9: 'And the anger of the Lord was kindled against him, and He departed.'

368. "What is this, 'And He departed'? Because the spirit of anger departed from those nostrils, and if he found any man before him, he was taken away, and was no more found.

369. "Which is intimated in these words, Isa. xl, 7: 'Because the Spirit of the Lord bloweth upon it.'

370. "But concerning Macroprosopus it is written: 'Passing over transgression.'

371. "Also it is written, Job xxxvii, 21: 'And the spirit (*wind*) passeth over and hath cleansed them.'

---

[5] This is simply a transposition of the two first letters of the word in question. Of course, the same letters being retained, though their relative places are changed, the numeration of the two words by Gematria will be identical. But it is worth our while to notice what the numeration of this word is, especially as Rabbi Chiya has not examined it. P + SH + O = 80 + 300 + 70 = 450 = THN, *Than,* the dragon. Ergo, according to the exegetical rule of Gematria, the dragon will be the symbol of transgression. But 450 is also the numeration of SHPO, influence: therefore is the dragon a symbol also of influence and of power. But "this influence passeth over into Microprosopus"; now one of the qabalistical axioms given by Pistorius is: "Paradise is the sephirotic tree. In the midst thereof the great Adam is Tiphereth." Therefore the influence passing over into Microprosopus is also the serpent entering into the garden of Eden.

372. "Also we have learned that on this account it is thus written: 'Passing over transgression' in that path. Also concerning that (*passage*), Exod. xii, 23: 'And He passeth over to smite the Egyptians.'

373. "Blessed is his portion who is worthy in this matter. And this is the third conformation of the path of the venerable, holy, and excellent beard of the Ancient of the Ancient Ones."

374. Rabbi Schimeon said unto him: "May God, the Holy One, blessed be He, be gracious unto thee, and protect thee most abundantly.

375. "Also we have learned: What is this which is written, 'With rejoicing will I rejoice in the Lord'? Concerning the Ancient of Days, is it said: 'For He is the praise of all things.'

376. "We have learned, whensoever that path of the beard of the Ancient of Days is manifested, all the authors of lamentation and mourning, and all the executors of judgment, are silent and hidden; nor is there one of them who openeth his mouth to do harm, because that path is manifested in due form.

377. "Hence also he who toucheth that mouth, and adviseth it to keep silence,[6] pointeth out this path with his finger; and that is the symbol denoting the Holy Ancient One." (Others read: Because that path is the symbol of silence; hence he who looked at another, and adviseth him to be silent, toucheth this path, which is the symbol, etc.)

[6] Meaning symbolically the idea of judgment.

CHAPTER XV

378. THE hair is disposed in the fourth conformation, and it descendeth beneath the mouth from the one side even unto the other side.

379. That is intimated *(in the saying of Micah)* in these words: "Of the remnant of his heritage:" *Lishairith Nachalatho.*

380. Like as it is said in 2 Kings xix, 4: "And thou shalt lift up thy prayer for the remnant that is left." Where every part that is found truly remaining is called the remnant.

381. For it is written, Zeph. iii. 13: "The remnant of Israel, *Sharith Israel*, shall not do iniquity."

CHAPTER XVI

CONCERNING THE FIFTH PART OF THE
BEARD OF MACROPROSOPUS

382. THE fifth conformation. Another path goeth forth beneath the mouth. This is that which is written in the saying of Micah: *"Lo Hecheziq Lead Apo,* He hath not kept his anger for ever." Arise! Rabbi Yosi!

383. Rabbi Yosi arose, and commencing said, Ps. cxliv, 15: " 'Blessed is the people that is in such a case; blessed is the people whose God is the Lord.'

384. "'Blessed is the people that is in such a case.' What is this *'Shekakah Lo,* That is in such a case'? Like as it is said in Est. vii, 10: 'And the wrath of the king was appeased,' *Shekakah;* that is, 'Became quiet from his wrathfulness.'

385. "Another exposition: He was appeased through his wrath, which is intimated in these words, Num. xi, 15: 'And if Thou dealest thus with me, kill me, I pray Thee, out of hand, if I have found grace in Thy sight.'

386. " 'Kill me, I pray Thee, out of hand'; this is judgment of judgments. But 'Blessed is the people whose God is the Lord'; this is mercy of mercies.

387. "Another exposition: *Shekaka,* is the name which includeth all names,[1] in consequence of which that Holy

---

[1] It is not at first sight evident why this word should be the "name which includeth all names." But if we examine it by Gematria we shall soon see the reason. ShKKH, SH + K + K + H = 300 + 20 + 20 + 5 = 345 = SHMH, *Shemah = Ha Shem,* The Name. This title Shemah is applied to the Lord frequently as being *the* name of all names, and therefore SHKKH is taken as concealing the Lord.

Blessed One maketh His wrath to pass away, and caused Microprosopus to be at peace, and taketh away all those extraneous (*matters*) from the midst.

388. "We have learned through Barietha (*or the tradition given forth without the holy city*), that that path of the conformation of the holy supernal Ancient of the Ancient Ones, which descendeth in the beard beneath the nostrils of the nose, and this inferior path, are equal in every way, in such a manner that that which is below is like that which is above.[2] The superior (*path*) is called 'passing over transgression'; the inferior, 'He hath not kept His anger for ever.'

389. "Also we have learned this: 'He hath not kept,' *i.e.*, there is no place *wherein anger* can remain. Like as in the superior there is opportunity given for taking away (*anger*), so also in the inferior is the (same opportunity) afforded.

390. "We have learned this: whensoever in this Ancient One, the most concealed of all, this path is uncovered, it is well for all the inferior (*paths*);[3] for then appeareth counsel for doing good to them all.

391. "But when it is withdrawn, and is not uncovered, there is no counsel, neither is there any who knoweth Him, save Himself.[4]

---

[2] Compare the precept in the Smaragdine tablet of Hermes Trismegistus: "That which is below is like that which is above, and that which is above is like that which is below, for the performance of the miracles of the one substance." This is the fundamental principle of all the ancient mystic doctrines, whether qabalistical, mythological, alchemical, or magical, and in this formula all are contained. As is God, so is the universe: as is the Creator the Supernal Man, so is the created the inferior man; as Macrocosm, so Microcosm; as eternity, so life!

[3] That is, the lower forms of the Sephiroth.

[4] Himself, *Hoa*, whom we can only symbolize by this pronoun; HE, who is the Absolute; HE, who is beyond us; that awful and unknowable Crown, who hath said, I AM; in Whom is neither past nor future, He Who is the ETERNAL PRESENT. Therefore is HE, *Hoa*, the Father, known of none

392. "Like as also none knoweth the superior Eden, save Himself, save Him, the Ancient of the Ancient Ones.

393. "And concerning this it is written, Ps. xcii, 6: 'O Lord, how excellent are Thy works! Thy thoughts are very deep!' "

394. Rabbi Schimeon said unto him: "May thy works be reckoned in order in the world to come by the Ancient of the Ancient Ones!"

---

save the Son, IHVH, and him to whom the Son will reveal Him. For none can see *Hoa* and live, for they would be absorbed in Him.

CHAPTER XVII

CONCERNING THE SIXTH PART OF THE BEARD OF MACROPROSOPUS

395. THE hair is arranged in the sixth conformation, and ascendeth from below upward, and toucheth the circles of most excellent fragrance, even unto the beginning of the mouth above; and the hair descendeth from the beginning (*of the mouth above*) unto the beginning of the opening of the mouth below. "Arise thou! Rabbi Yisa, and expound this conformation."

396. Rabbi Yisa arose, and commenced, and said, Is. liv, 10: "'And thy blessing shall not depart from thee!'

397. "Also it is written: 'And in everlasting compassion have I had mercy upon thee.'

398. "Do not these verses contradict one another? They do not. For this is what we have learned: there is given a compassion (*of one kind*), and again there is given a compassion of another kind. For the one is the interior compassion, and the other is the external compassion.

399. "The interior compassion is that of which we have spoken concerning the Ancient of Days, and that is concealed in this part of the beard, which is called the angle of the beard.

400. "Neither is it advisable for a man to destroy this part (*of his beard*) because of this interior compassion of the Ancient of Days.

401. "And therefore is it written concerning the inferior priesthood, Lev. xxi, 5: 'They shall not make baldness upon

their head, neither shall they shave off the angle of their beard.'

402. "Wherefore? Lest they should destroy the path of the Mercy of the Ancient One. For also the priesthood is (*symbolically*) referred unto this path.

403. "Also we have learned in the 'Book of Concealed Mystery' that every work existeth in order that it may procure increase for Mercy, and that it may establish the same; also that this is not to be cut off nor removed from the world.

404. "This is that which is written: 'And My Compassion shall not depart from thee.' Namely, the Compassion of the Ancient of Days.

405. "*(But when it is said in another text,)* 'And in mercy, Olahm, for ever' *(this is the sense)*, the mercy which is called 'mercy for ever' is the second form concerning which it is written, Ps. lxxxix, 2: 'I have said, Mercy shall be built up for ever.'

406. "And this compassion of the Ancient of Days is the mercy of truth. And *(this phrase)* 'mercy of truth' is not said concerning the life of the body, but concerning the life of the soul.

407. "And therefore is it written, Mic. vii, 18: 'Since He Himself wisheth Mercy.' This is the sixth conformation of the venerable beard of the Ancient of the Ancient Ones."

CHAPTER XVIII

CONCERNING THE SEVENTH PART OF THE BEARD OF MACROPROSOPUS

408. THE seventh conformation is that wherein the hair is wanting, and there appear two apples in the circles of fragrance, fair and beautiful of aspect.

409. Rabbi Schimeon commenced, and said, Cant. ii, 3: " 'Like as the apple-tree among the trees of the wood, so is my beloved among the sons.'

410. "What is the apple-tree? Like as this in itself hath three colors, so do the two apples of the holy blessed one contain six colors.

411. "And those two apples which are the seventh conformation include all the six conformations before mentioned.

412. "And concerning them is that passage (*to be taken in*), Prov. xvi, 15: 'In the light of the countenance of the King is life.'

413. "Also we have learned that from those apples goeth forth the life of the universe, and it giveth joy unto Microprosopus; like as it is written, Num. vi, 24: 'The Lord maketh His countenance to shine upon thee.'

414. "And it is written: 'In the light of the countenance of the King is life.' 'In the light of the countenance of the King.' Those are the two apples of the circles of fragrance of which we have spoken.

415. " 'The Lord make His countenance to shine upon

thee.' Here is understood the exterior countenance which when it shineth blesseth the universe.

416. "And we have learned that whensoever those external lights shine He blesseth the whole world, and wrath is no longer found in the universe.

417. "And if these externals (*do this*), how much more do these two apples, which ever shine, which ever are joyful!

418. "This is a tradition, given forth without the city.[1] 'When those two apples are disclosed, Microprosopus appeareth in joy; for all those inferior lights are joyful; and all those inferiors shine; and all the worlds rejoice, and are perfected in all perfection; and all things rejoice and shine, and no good thing is wanting; all things are satisfied at once; all things rejoice together at the same time.'

419. "Come, behold! The external countenance at times shineth, at times is obscured; and therefore is it written: 'The Lord make His face to shine upon thee.' And, Ps. i.: 'And cause His face to shine upon us. Selah.'

420. "Whence (*we learn*), that it is not always (*luminous*), but only when those superior apples are uncovered.

421. "This have we learned by tradition. 'Those hidden apples shine, and are ever brilliant; and from them proceed rays in three hundred and seventy[2] directions; and in them all the six (*preceding*) conformations of the beard are included.'

422. "This is that which is said, Mic. vii, 18: 'May He return and have mercy upon us!' May He return, that is, again;[3] whence it is to be noticed that sometimes they are

---

[1] I suppose this means later than the Captivity.

[2] 370 = OSH, *Aush* = formation, action, creation. And the least number of 3 + 70 = 37 = 10 = Malkuth, the decad of the Sephiroth.

[3] Expressed by the *re* in *re*turn.

concealed and sometimes uncovered; wherefore it is said: 'May He return and have mercy upon us!'

423. "And in that which is inferior (*correspondeth to this form*) the name, *Amath*, Truth. This is the seventh conformation, which includeth the six first, in the two apples of the Ancient of the Ancient Ones."

CHAPTER XIX

CONCERNING THE EIGHTH PART OF THE BEARD OF MACROPROSOPUS

424. THE eighth conformation. There goeth forth a certain tress of hairs surrounding the beard, and they hang down evenly into the heart. "Arise thou, Eleazar, my son, and expound this conformation."

425. Rabbi Eleazar, his son, arose, and commenced, and said: "All things depend from the influx, even the Book of the Law in the Temple. This have we understood from the 'Book of Concealed Mystery,' and it speaketh thus.

426. "Therefore do not then all things depend from the influx? Also we have learned that the Book of the Law must be holy, and its covering holy, and the Temple holy.

427. "Also it is written, Isa. vi, 4: 'And they called one unto another and said: Holy, holy, holy!' Behold these three (*repetitions of the word 'holy'*) unto which the Book of the Law correspondeth, for its covering is holy, and the Temple is holy, and the book itself is holy.

428. "And thus the law hath been constructed in triple holiness, in three degrees, in three days, (*but*) the Schechinah (*is*) in the three (*following*) which are the Table, the Ark, and the Temple; and in the same manner it dependeth from the Book of the Law, and that dependeth from the Influx.

429. "Also it is written, Jer. x, 2: 'Be ye not dismayed at the signs (*or influences*) of the heavens.' Because if they exist

in holiness, in the same way they must depend from the Influx.

430. But thus have we read in the "Book of Concealed Mystery" that this venerable holy tress of hair, wherein all the locks of the beard hang down, is called the Influx. Wherefore? Because that all the holinesses of the holinesses of all holinesses depend from that Influx.

431. "And in the Book of the Law, although it is holy, the ten holinesses[1] do not descend, until it be brought into the Temple. But after that it is brought into the Temple it is called holy with the ten holinesses.

432. "As in the above instance mention is not made of the Temple save when the ten holinesses are associated with it.

433. "Also we have learned that all things depend from that Influx which is (*symbolized by*) that tress of (hair of the beard) from which all (*the other*) hairs depend.

434. "Why is this called the Influx (*or influence*)? Because from it depend the influences and the influences of the influences, and from it come forth those which are above and those which are below.

435. "And because it dependeth, and that in it all the things of the universe depend, superiors and inferiors; also in the last place the Book of the Law, which is in the Temple, and is crowned with the ten holinesses, is not excepted

---

[1] This of course refers to the ten Sephiroth. In the *Sepher Yetzirah*, a very ancient and mystical qabalistical book attributed to Abraham the Patriarch, which treats of the creation of the universe through the symbolism of the ten numbers (*Sephiroth*), and the twenty-two letters, together called the thirty-two paths of wisdom, where the ten numbers are derived into a tetrad and a hexed (the latter consisting of the four cardinal points of the compass, together with height and depth), this phrase is employed: "And in the midst of the hexad is the Holy Temple."

hence with the other holinesses. All things depend from it (*this conformation, namely*).

436. "And he who beholdeth that form, before him are they subjected and inflected (others read: *'all sins are subjected, etc.'*) according to that which is written: *'Yekebosh Auonothino*, He hath pardoned our iniquities' (*or He hath subjected, etc.*)."

437. Rabbi Schimeon said unto him: "O my son! blessed be thou by the Holy of the Holy Ones, the One Ancient before all."

CHAPTER XX

CONCERNING THE NINTH PART OF THE BEARD OF MACROPROSOPUS

438. THE ninth conformation. The hairs are mingled with those hairs that hang down, neither is one preeminent above another. "Arise, Rabbi Abba!"

439. Rabbi Abba arose and said: "These are the hairs which are mingled with these which hang down, and they are called 'the deep places of the sea,' because they depart from above in the fluid places of the brain.

440. "And from that place are cast out all the lords who are the exactors of the debts (*of the trespasses*) of mankind, and they are subjugated."

441. Rabbi Schimeon said unto him: "Blessed be thou of the Ancient of Days!"

CHAPTER XXI

CONCERNING THE TENTH AND ELEVENTH PARTS OF THE BEARD OF MACROPROSOPUS

442. THE tenth conformation. The hairs descend beneath the beard, and cover the throat beneath the beard. "Arise, Rabbi Yehuda."

443. Rabbi Yehuda arose, and commenced, and said, Isa. ii, 19: " 'And they shall enter into the holes of the rocks, and into the caves of the earth, from the countenance of the terror of the Lord of Hosts, and from the glory of His Majesty, when he shall arise to shake terribly the earth.'

444. "'From the countenance of the Terror[1] of the Lord.' It is to be carefully noted that that which is exterior is called the Terror of the Lord.

445. "'And from the Glory of His Majesty.' These are the hairs beneath the beard, and they are called the Glory of His Majesty.

446. "*(But)* these two *(conformations agree with)* §§ 268, 269, *ante)*; the tenth with 'Thou shalt give truth unto Jacob.'

447. "And the eleventh, because one hair is not preeminent over another hair, with 'mercy unto Abraham.' "

---

[1] *Pachad,* Terror, is a title of the fifth Sephira, Geburah, Strength, to which the divine name of Elohim Gibor, the Elohim of Strength, is referred. It is likewise to be remembered that from this Sephira the Pillar of Justice takes its title, which includes the third, fifth, and eighth Sephiroth; Binah, Geburah, and Hod; Understanding, Strength or Terror, and Splendor. Mars, "the star of the unconquered will," is also referred to this fifth Sephira.

CHAPTER XXII

CONCERNING THE TWELFTH PART OF THE BEARD OF MACROPROSOPUS

448. THE twelfth conformation is that the hairs do not hang over the mouth, and that the mouth is bare on every part, and that beautiful are the hairs surrounding it, so that there may be no molestation there, as is fit.

449. But wherein consisteth the molestation? Doubtless it is frequently said, "If judgment exist in the place of judgment (or, If judgment follow after judgment), molestation ariseth."

450. Therefore are the hairs of the beard either (*symbolical of*) molestation or judgment, while the other parts appear to (symbolize) mercy.

451. Surely it is said for this reason, because the breathings forth of the Spirit upon Microprosopus are not molestations.

452. For we have learned that from that holy and excellent mouth of the Holy of the Holy Ones the Spirit breaketh forth.

453. What spirit? The Spirit which floweth forth upon Microprosopus, that it may enshroud Him.

454. And with that Spirit are all those[1] veiled which are inferior. And when that Spirit goeth forth, then is it divided

---

[1] That is, the fourth, fifth, sixth, seventh, eighth, and ninth Sephiroth which form Microprosopus; and the tenth, which is the Bride.

into 37,000 aspects,[2] of which each one is expanded, but only in its proper place.

455. And he who is worthy to be enshrouded is enshrouded by (*the Spirit*).

456. And therefore hairs are not found upon the holy mouth, because thence the Spirit rusheth forth; neither is it necessary that any (*extraneous things*) whatsoever should be mingled therewith or approach thereto.

457. And that (*mouth*) is very secret, because to it nothing adhereth, nor doth anything touch upon it from above or below; and it is concealed in the secret of secrets, so that it cannot be known.

458. In fact, it is not formed, nor doth it exist[3] (properly speaking) in this conformation.

459. And because that Spirit which proceedeth unto the exteriors, and wherewith the true prophets have been overshadowed, is called the mouth of the Lord.

460. But herein, in the Ancient of the Ancient Ones, is it not made manifest, nor is there any who knoweth His Spirit save Himself.

461. And therefore are the hairs of (*the beard*) of equal length around the mouth; and this latter is bare in every part.

462. And herein have our fathers put their trust, that they might be overshadowed by that Spirit which is developed in multitudinous aspects, each in its proper place, wherewith all the equal hairs are surrounded.

463. This is that which is written in that passage of Micah: "Which thou has sworn unto our fathers."

---

[2] That is, 37 in the material, or Asiah = ZL, *Zal* = profession, or LZ, *Laz* = diversion of force.

[3] Meaning that in this place it is the conformations of the *beard* and not the *mouth* that are being described.

464. And this is the holy and excellent twelfth conformation, from which, linked together, depend twelve limitations above and twelve limitations below; even twelve limitations, according unto the twelve tribes of our fathers.

465. This is that which is written: "Which Thou hast sworn unto our fathers."

CHAPTER XXIII

CONCERNING THE THIRTEENTH PART OF THE BEARD OF MACROPROSOPUS

466. THE thirteenth conformation. The hairs which are beneath the beard hang down on this side and on that in beautiful and excellent dignity, and form a covering even unto the chest, and nothing is seen of the countenance and of the places of fragrance save those two brilliant and beautiful apples.

467. Rabbi Schimeon spake and said: "O how blessed is his portion who is found in this excellent holy assembly,[1] wherein we are (*assembled*)! Blessed is his portion in this world and in the world to come.

468. "For we are seated in that excellent holiness which surroundeth us.

469. "And all those excellent conformations are coordinated, and crowned, and placed round about, each in its own (*proper*) position, in the holy form of the beard.

470. "And this thirteenth disposition is the beautiful disposition which exciteth in itself so great desire that the head[2] ariseth toward it.

[1] Because this assembly of ten Rabbis, as I have before remarked, was intended to typify the ten Sephiroth and their grouping.

[2] This somewhat obscure text means this: The number of the parts of the beard are 13, which are now completed in this disposition. But 13 = ACHD, *Achad*, Unity, and also AHBH, *Ahebah*, Love. Hence love of unity ariseth when the 13 are complete. And the head of Macroprosopus ariseth, because that is Kether, the first Sephira, the number one, unity.

471. "From it depend all those which are comprehended in Microprosopus; from it depend alike those which are supernal, those which are inferior.

472. "This is the form of perfection which consummateth all the dispositions, and which perfecteth all things.

473. "We have learned by tradition. Those parts[3] are called *Qadam*,[4] ancient days, days first of the first. But those which are found in Microprosopus are called *Olahm*, everlasting days, or days of the ages.

474. "Also we have learned that those *Qadam*, ancient days, are all conformed in the conformations of the beard, wherein is composed the Ancient of the Ancient Ones, the Concealed of the Concealed Ones. But this thirteenth (*conformation*) comprehendeth them.[5]

475. "And all the concealed superiors and inferiors are concealed in it, and they are comprehended in that Influx from which all things emanate; like as it is said:

476. "And that day is not comprehended in them, seeing it comprehendeth all things.

477. "And in that time wherein is stirred up the Ancient of Days in the superior conformations, that is called one day wherein He ariseth to magnify His beard.

478. "Which is intimated in those words, Zech. xiv, 7: 'One day which is known to the Lord.'

479. "That alone prevaileth over all, that includeth all things that is called by the known name.

---

[3] That is, the thirteen conformations of the beard.

[4] And hence is Macroprosopus called the "Ancient of Days." Qadam also means the east, eastward. The Lord Elohim planted a garden, MQDM, *Migedem*, eastward (or of ancient time), in Eden. It is worthy of notice that the Gematria of QDM and OVLM are 144 and 146 respectively; the least numbers of which are 9 and 2—Yesod and Chokmah, foundation and wisdom.

[5] By way of synthesis, as if it were a repetition of the rest conjointly.

480. "For thus we have learned. In that place where there is day there is also night, seeing that day cannot exist without night.

481. "But because in that time shall be the time of the dignity of the beard, that day is found alone.

482. "It is called neither day nor night, for it is not called day except for our (*better understanding of the symbolism involved*), neither is it called night except for the same reason.

483. "And because that form includeth all things, hence nothing whatsoever is known or seen concerning it.

484. "And from it streameth down the oil of magnificence in thirteen directions, which flow down upon all the inferiors in order that they may shine forth.

485. "In that oil are consummated the thirteen parts of the holy and excellent beard.

486. "And those forms which are in that beard are disposed and descend in many directions, neither can it be seen how they are extended nor how they arise.

487. "They are hidden in all things, and they are concealed in all things; and no man knoweth their place, except Him, the Ancient One.

488. "In their expansion are they all included, like as it is said:

489. "He is known, and He is not known; He is concealed, and He is manifest.

490. "Concerning Him it is written. Isa. xlii, 8: '*Ani the Lord Hoa,*[6] This is My name, and My glory I give not unto another.'

---

[6] There are 10 letters in this phrase = 10 Sephiroth. "Ani the Lord Hoa, This is My name"; for in this are contained Macroprosopus, Microprosopus and the Lord. ANI represents Microprosopus; HVA represents Macroprosopus and is also ABA the Father; and IHVH is between them. Ani is 61 and ABA is 4 which together give 65, which is ADNI, *Adonai,* Lord, and IHVH = 26, which added hereunto is 91 = AMN, *Amen.* Now,

491. "Also it is written, Ps. c, 2: *'Hoa*, He, hath made us, and not we ourselves.'

492. "Also it is written, Dan. vii, 9: 'The Ancient of Days did sit,' that is, He remained in His place, and Him hath no man known. He sitteth, but He is not found.

493. "Also it is written, Ps. cxxxix, 14: 'I will praise Thee, for I am fearfully and wonderfully made.' "

---

apart from the sacred ideas we attach to Amen, it is well to know that the ancient Egyptians called their greatest Deity *Amen*, AMN, Amen-Ra, and Ra = Light, AVR in Hebrew; Amen our Light, the light of the two countenances.

CHAPTER XXIV
CONCLUSION OF THE MATTER CONCERNING MACROPROSOPUS

494. RABBI SCHIMEON spake unto his companions, and said: "When that veil is expanded (*by which is to be understood the representation of the beard of Macroprosopus*) which ye behold above us,[1] I see that all the conformations have descended therein, and that they shine forth in that place. (*Now like as if he intended to say, Amen, the discourse concerning Macroprosopus being finished, he describeth this particular symbolism, which is contained in the ensuing symbols.*)

495. "And a certain covering, even the splendor of the most holy and blessed God (*otherwise the opening of holiness; but by this is understood the Lord, which, together with the name, Adonai, maketh the number of the word, Amen, that is 91*): is expanded through four columns on four sides (*which are the four letters of the holy name, by which he saith that space is surrounded*).

496. "One column is so placed that it reacheth from the lowest unto the highest. (*This is the Kingdom of the emanations,[2] the base and lowest part of the whole system[3] of emanation,*

---

[1] Again alluding to their symbolical representation of the ten Sephiroth.

[2] Malkuth, the tenth Sephira.

[3] The Sephiroth.

*because it is said to ascend from the lowest part of the middle col-
umn[4] even unto the summit of the Crown.[5]*)

497. "And therein is a certain *Megerophia*,[6] vessel containing fire (*for like as the fire on the altar could not be touched with
bare hands, so that name, the Lord, cannot be touched and pronounced by the mouth, but it is touched and produced by Adonai,
which is Sham, His name; for SHM and MGRVPIA both yield
340 by Gematria*); and in the fire-containing vessel are four
keys,[7] sharp on every side (*for such was the form of the keys, in
order that they might draw aside the veil, as a lock is shot back by
a key. But the four letters of the name Adonai are hereby to be understood, which are inserted into and united with the four letters
IHVH, in this manner, IAHDVNHI*); which seize upon that
veil, and withdraw it from the superiors.

498. "And thus in the second column,[8] and the third column and the fourth column (*that is, the four letters are applied
to the other four letters, as hath just been said*).

499. "And between one column and another column are
contained eighteen[9] bases of columns (*here is to be under-*

---

[4] Or Pillar of Mildness, consisting of the first, sixth, ninth, and tenth
Sephiroth.

[5] Kether. "Malkuth is Kether after another manner," says one of the
qabalistic axioms of Pistorius.

[6] I believe the best translation of Megerophia is a "fire shovel." Knorr
von Rosenroth makes it "uncus focarius."

[7] Quatuor craves traditæ sunt in manu Domini mundi, quas non tra-
didit neque ulli Angelo, neque seraphino: clavis pluviæ: clavis sustenta-
tionis: clavis sepulchorum: clavis sterilitatis, &c. (Zanolini: "Lexicon
Chaldæo-Rabbinicum," art. MPThCh, root PThCh.)

[8] These four columns also refer to the four worlds of Atziloth, Briah,
Yetzirah, and Asiah.

[9] 18 = CHI = Life.

stood the name expounded through the seventy-two[10] *names or numbers; for either pertain unto Macroprosopus, and four times eighteen yieldeth seventy-two*): and they shine forth with brilliancy in the openings carved out in that veil, and so on all four sides. (*By the "openings carved out" is to be understood the exposition of the name, the Lord.*)

500. "I beheld those forms which shine above it, and await the words of our lips, that they may be crowned and raised each in its own place.

501. "And when they are expounded by our lips, they ascend singly and are crowned, and are disposed in that order which is here given forth by the mouth of whosoever amongst us (*happeneth to be expounding them*).

502. "And whensoever anyone amongst us openeth his mouth, so that he may speak concerning any conformation, that form is localized and awaiteth the voice which goeth forth from our lips, and then it ascendeth in its place and is crowned.

503. "And all the columns on this side and on that side rejoice (*here are understood the holy living creatures, the cherubim, which were before the columns, and the chiefs of the angelic guards, and they are said to have come hither*); because they

---

[10] In Exodus xiv are three verses (19, 20, and 21), which each consist of 72 letters. Now, if these three verses be written at length one above another, the first from right to left, the second from left to right, and the third from right to left (or, as the Greeks would say, *boustrophedon*), they will give 72 columns of three letters each. Then each column will be a word of three letters, and as there are 72 columns, there will be 72 words of three letters, each of which will be the 72 names of the Deity alluded to in the text. And these are called the Schemahamphorasch, or the divided name. By writing the verses all from right to left, instead of *boustrophedon*, etc., there will be other sets of 72 names obtainable. (See annexed Table of the Schemahamphorasch.)

THE SCHEMAHAMPHORASCH

Div.	No.			
I	1	V	H	V
	2	I	L	I
	3	S	I	T
	4	O	L	M
	5	M	H	Sh
	6	L	L	H
	7	A	K	A
	8	K	H	Th
	9	H	Z	I
	10	A	L	D
	11	L	A	V
	12	H	H	O
	13	I	Z	L
	14	M	B	H
	15	H	R	I
	16	H	Q	M
	17	L	A	V
	18	K	L	I
H	19	L	V	O
	20	P	H	L
	21	N	L	K
	22	I	I	I
	23	M	L	H
	24	Ch	H	V
	25	N	Th	H
	26	H	A	A
	27	I	R	Th
	28	Sh	A	H
	29	R	I	I
	30	O	M	M
	31	L	K	B
	32	V	Sh	R
	33	I	Ch	V
	34	L	H	Ch
	35	K	V	Q
	36	M	N	D
V	37	A	N	I
	38	Ch	O	M
	39	R	H	O
	40	I	I	Z
	41	H	H	H
	42	M	I	K
	43	V	V	L
	44	I	L	H
	45	S	A	L
	46	O	R	I
	47	O	Sh	L
	48	M	I	H
	49	V	H	V
	50	D	N	I
	51	H	Ch	Sh
	52	O	M	M
	53	N	N	A
	54	N	I	Th
H	55	M	B	H
	56	P	V	I
	57	N	M	M
	58	I	I	L
	59	H	R	Ch
	60	M	Tz	R
	61	V	M	B
	62	I	H	H
	63	O	N	V
	64	M	Ch	I
	65	D	M	B
	66	M	N	Q
	67	A	I	O
	68	Ch	B	V
	69	R	A	H
	70	I	B	M
	71	H	I	I
	72	M	V	M

(If to each of these trilateral names AL or IH, El or Yah, be added, the names of 72 Angels are obtained, who rule over the 72 quinaries of the degrees of the Zodiac.)

1. Vehu; 2. Yeli; 3. Sit; 4. Aulem; 5. Mahash; 6. Lelah; 7. Aka; 8. Kahath; 9. Hezi; 10. Elad; 11. Lav; 12. Hahau; 13. Yezel; 14. Mebah; 15. Heri; 16. Haqem; 17. Lau; 18. Keli; 19. Levo; 20. Pahel; 21. Nelak; 22. Yiai; 23. Melah; 24. Chaho; 25. Nethah; 26. Haa; 27. Yereth; 28. Shaah; 29. Riyi; 30. Aum; 31. Lekab; 32. Vesher; 33. Yecho; 34. Lehach; 35. Keveq; 36. Menad; 37. Ani; 38. Chaum; 39. Rehau; 40. Yeiz; 41. Hahah; 42. Mik; 43. Veval; 44. Yelah; 45. Sael; 46. Auri; 47. Aushal; 48. Miah; 49. Vaho; 50. Doni; 51. Hachash; 52. Aumem; 53. Nena; 54. Neith; 55. Mabeh; 56. Poï; 57. Nemem; 58. Yeil; 59. Harach; 60. Metzer; 61. Vamet; 62. Yehah; 63. Aunu; 64. Mechi; 65. Dameb; 66. Menaq; 67. Aiau; 68. Chebo; 69. Raah; 70. Yebem; 71. Haiai; 72. Möum.

hear that which before they knew not.[11] And in the sound of your voices are heard the rushing of countless chariots (*the noise of the wings of the hosts of the angelic chariots of God, rushing onward*); and they stand here around you in multitudes, awaiting the speech of your voice.

504. "O blessed are ye in the world to come! because all the words which go forth from your mouth are all holy, all true, which err not, neither on the right nor yet on the left (*seeing they are the holy names of God*).

505. "God, the holy and blessed one, rejoiceth to hear these things, and He listeneth unto these words until He himself shall give sentence, for in the world to come all these holy words shall be enumerated for the second time.

506. "Concerning you is it written, Cant. vii, 9: 'And the roof of thy mouth, like the best wine for my beloved, that goeth down sweetly, causing the lips of those that are asleep to speak.'

507. "What is this? 'Causing the lips of those that are asleep to speak.' Because even in the world to come shall your lips utter the words of the law before Him."

---

[11] I must again remind the reader that Rabbi Schimeon and his companions are speaking as symbolizing the action of the Sephiroth in the creation, and that when it is said the angels, etc., wait for the words from their lips, it signifies symbolically the way in which the angels, etc., were created by the word of the Deity in his Sephirotic form. And when it is said that "they hear that which before they knew not," it signifies the creation of forms, powers, and attributes which at the beginning of time existed not.

CHAPTER XXV

The Ingress of Microprosopus

508. "Now take ye your places, and apply the science (*the Qabalah*) to describe how the parts of Microprosopus are conformed, and how He is clothed with His conformations, from the forms of the Ancient of Days, the Holy of the Holy Ones, the Withdrawn of the Withdrawn ones, the Concealed one of All.

509. "For now wisdom requireth that ye judge a true judgment, becoming and honorable; so that ye may dispose all the conformations as accurately as possible.

510. "But the conformations of Microprosopus are disposed from the forms of Macroprosopus; and his constituent parts are expanded on this side and on that under a human form, so that there may be manifest in Him the Spirit of the Concealed One in every part.

511. "So that He may be placed upon His throne, because it is written, Ezek. i, 26: 'And above the likeness of a throne, the appearance as the likeness of a man upon it above.'

512. "'Like as the appearance of a man'; because that (form) includeth all forms. 'Like as the appearance of a man'; because He includeth all names. 'Like as the appearance of a man.' Because He includeth all secret things which have been said or propounded before the world was created, even although they have not been substituted herein."[1]

---

[1] This brings in the subject of the worlds of unbalanced force which are said by the Zohar to have been created and destroyed prior to the creation of the present world. These worlds of unbalanced force are typified by the Edomite kings. ·

CHAPTER XXVI

CONCERNING THE EDOMITE KINGS

513. BEHOLD! this have we learned in the "Book of Concealed Mystery": that the Ancient of the Ancient Ones before that He prepared His conformations[1] (*in the equilibrium of balance*) formed certain kings, collected certain kings, and gave due proportion unto certain kings; but they only subsisted (*for a time*) until He could expel them; and in that time hath He concealed them.

514. This is intimated in those words, Gen. xxxvi, 31: "And these are the kings which have reigned in *Edom*."[2] In the land of Edom; that is, in the place wherein all judgments exist.

515. But all these subsisted not until the White Head[3] of the Ancient of the Ancient Ones was disposed (*in its ordination*).

516. When this was conformed, He disposed all the infe-

---

[1] As the Sephiroth proceed each from the preceding one in the series, it is evident that before the counterbalancing Sephira is formed, the force in the preceding Sephira is unbalanced; *e.g.*, the fourth Sephira is Gedulah or Chesed, Mercy; and the fifth Sephira is Geburah or Pachad, Sternness: therefore, till Geburah appears, Gedulah is unbalanced, and this condition is the reign of one of the Edomite kings; but when Geburah appears, his reign is over.

[2] ADVM = 1 + 4 + 6 + 40 = 51 = NA = Failure. AN = also 51, and means pain. *Ergo*, also unbalanced force is the source alike of failure and of pain.

[3] This is another title of the Crown, Kether, the first Sephira.

rior conformations, and all the superior and inferior forms were thus arranged.

517. Thence we learn that unless the head (*or ruling power, or government*) of a nation, whatever form of government it may happen to be, be first properly constituted, that nation cannot be properly ruled. For if the head be first disposed aright, then all things can be ordained, but if that be not first disposed aright, neither can the nation be governed aright.

518. The ordering of all things is from the Ancient of Days. For before that He was disposed in His conformation, nothing could be ordained, because as yet it was first necessary that Himself [4] should be ordained; and all the worlds were desolate.

519. Which these words intimate, *ibid.* 32: "And there reigned in Edom Bela, the son of Beor."

520. "And there reigned in Edom." Here is a certain venerable Arcanum hidden; for herein is that place intimated wherein all the judgments are collected together, and whence they depend.

521. "Bela, the son of Beor." This is the tradition. This denoteth the most rigorous judicial decree, for whose cause there are collected together a thousand times a thousand authors of mourning and woe.

522. "And the name of his city is Dinhabah." What is *Dinhabah?* As if it were to be said, "Give forth judgment." Like as it is written, Prov. xxx, 15: "The horseleech hath two daughters, crying, 'Give, give.' "

523. But when he ascendeth, so that he may be conformed therein, he cannot subsist and he cannot consist. Wherefore? Because the form of the man is not as yet constituted.

---

[4] Because He is the Absolute One, the Eheieh Asher Eheieh.

524. What is the reason of this? Because the constitution of man containeth all things under this form, and in that form are all things disposed.

525. And because that constitution of Adam was not as yet found, they (*the Edomite Kings*) could not subsist, nor be conformed, and they were destroyed.

526. Have they then been abolished, and are all these included in (*the supernal*) man? For truly they were abolished that they might be withdrawn from form, until there should come forth the representation of Adam.

527. But when that form is configurated, they all exist, and have been restored in another condition.

528. Some among them are mitigated, and (*some*) are not mitigated; but evidently there are certain of them which have not been mitigated.

529. And if thou shalt say: "Also it is written, 'and he died,' surely that denoteth that they were altogether abolished." I answer that it is not so; but whosoever descendeth from his former position wherein he was before, concerning such an one is it said in Scripture that he died.

530. Like as it is written, Exod. ii, 23: "And the King of Egypt died." Because he descended from the former condition wherein he was.

531. But after that Adam was constituted they are called by other names, and are mitigated in a permanent condition through him; and they exist in their place, and are all called by other names and not by their former (*appellations*).

532. Excepting that one[5] concerning whom it is written, Gen. xxxvi, 39: "And the name of his wife was Mehetabel, the daughter of Matred, the daughter of Mezahab."

533. For what reason? Because they were not abolished like the others. Wherefore? Because they were male and fe-

[5] Hadar.

male, like as the palm-tree, which groweth not unless there be both male and female.

534. And because now they are found male and female, and it is not written concerning them that they died like as the others, but remained in a fixed condition.

535. But they were not (*definitely composed*) until the form of the man was composed (*that is, the supernal man*). But after that the form of the supernal Adam was constituted, they were restored in another condition, and came in proper order.

CHAPTER XXVII

CONCERNING THE SKULL OF MICROPROSOPUS AND
ITS APPURTENANCES; NAMELY, CONCERNING
THE SUBTLE AIR, AND THE FIRE,
AND THE DEW

536. THIS is the tradition. When the White Head[1] propounded unto Himself to superadd ornament unto His own adornment, He constituted, prepared, and produced one single spark from His intense splendor of light. He fanned it and condensed it (or conformed it).

537. And He developed His thought, and extended it in three hundred and seventy directions.

538. And the spark subsisted, and waited until the pure air went forth which involved it around; and an ultimate extension having been made, He produced a certain hard skull (*bounded*) on four sides.[2]

539. And in that pure subtle air was the spark absorbed and comprehended and included therein.

540. Dost thou not think therein? Truly it is hidden therein.

541. And therefore is that skull expanded in its sides; and that air is the most concealed attribute of the Ancient of Days.

542. In the spirit which is hidden in that skull there are expanded fire on the one side and air on the other. And the

[1] Another title for the crown, Kether.
[2] By the letters of the Tetragram.

subtle air is whirled about it from this side, and the subtle fire is whirled about it from that side.

543. What is the fire in this place? But verily it is not fire, but that splendor which is included in the subtle air, and it shineth in two hundred and seventy worlds.

544. And rigor or judgment is found therefrom; and therefore it is called the hard skull.

545. Within that skull are nine thousand myriads of worlds, which receive the influx from it, and are at peace above it.

546. In that skull distilleth the dew[3] from the White Head, which is ever filled therewith; and from that dew are the dead raised unto life.

547. And that dew hath in itself two colors. From the White Head there is a whiteness in it, which entirely comprehendeth all whiteness.

548. But whensoever it remaineth in that head of Microprosopus, there appeareth in it a redness, like as in crystal, which is white, and there appeareth a red color in the white color.

549. And therefore is it written, Dan. xii, 2: "And many of them that sleep in the dust of the earth shall awake, some to everlasting life, and some to shame and everlasting contempt."

550. "To everlasting life." Because they are worthy of that whiteness which cometh from Macroprosopus, even from the Ancient of Days.

551. "To shame and everlasting contempt." Because they are worthy of that redness of Microprosopus.

552. And all things are contained in that dew as is inti-

---

[3] This subtle air, fire, and dew are analogous to the three "mother letters" of the *Sepher Yetzirah,* A, M, and SH; the letter A symbolizing air, the medium between M the water, and SH the fire.

mated in these words, Isa. xxvi, 19: "Because the dew of lights is thy dew"—where there is a duality of expression.

553. And that dew, which distilleth, distilleth daily upon the field of apples, in color white and red.

554. This skull shineth in two colors toward this side and toward that.

555. And from that subtle air, from the skull, there are expanded in His countenance one hundred and fifty myriads of worlds; and therefore is He called Zauir Aphin (or Anpin), Microprosopus, the Lesser Countenance.

556. But in that time, when there is need, is His countenance expanded and made vast, because He looketh back upon the countenance of the Ancient of the Ancient Ones, from whom is the life of the universe.

557. And from that skull there is a place of exit in one place unto those which are below; and they reflect His light toward the Ancient of Days, when they ascend in numeration beneath the wand.[4]

558. Therefore is His skull cleft beneath, when (the inferiors) ascend in numeration, and from this cleavage a reflection of light ariseth toward the Ancient of Days.

---

[4] This statement will be utterly unintelligible to the ordinary reader, unless he is told that there are four secret qabalistical symbols attached to the four letters of the Lord—*viz.*, the wand to I, the cup of libation to H, the sword to V and the shekel of gold to H final. The wand in the text refers to the I, *Yod*, of the Ancient One, hidden and concealed in the I of IHVH, and at the head of the Sephiroth.

CHAPTER XXVIII

CONCERNING THE BRAIN AND MEMBRANE
OF THE BRAIN OF MICROPROSOPUS

559. In the cavities of the skull three hollow places are found wherein is located the brain.

560. And a thin membrane is placed therein, but not a thick membrane, hidden also as that of the Ancient of Days.

561. And therefore is this brain expanded, and it shineth (or proceedeth) in thirty-two[1] paths. The same is that which is written, Gen. ii, 7: "And a river went forth out of Eden."

562. Also we have learned that in the three hollow places of the skull the brain is contained.

563. Out of the first cavity proceedeth a certain fountain of the brain in four directions, and it goeth forth from the skull, in whose cavity are contained those thirty-two paths which are the spirits of wisdom.

564. Out of the second cavity there goeth forth and expandeth a second certain fountain, and the fifty gates (*of the Understanding*) are opened.

565. In those fifty gates are contained the fifty days of the law; the fifty years of the jubilee; and the fifty thousand generations wherein the most holy God—blessed be He!—intendeth to restore and commemorate His Spirit in them.

566. From the third cavity there go forth a thousand times

---

[1] These are the thirty-two paths of the *Sepher Yetzirah*, symbolized by the ten numbers of the decad, and the twenty-two letters of the Hebrew alphabet.

a thousand conclaves and assemblies, wherein *Daath*,[2] Knowledge, is contained and dwelleth.

567. And the hollow place of this cavity is placed between the other two cavities;[3] and all those conclaves are filled from either side.

568. This is that which is written, Prov. ii, 4: "And in knowledge shall the conclaves be filled."

569. And those three are expanded over the whole body, on this side and on that, and with them doth the whole body cohere, and the body is contained by them on every side, and through the whole body are they expanded and diffused.

---

[2] It is to be remembered that, according to the "Book of Concealed Mystery," Daath is the conjunction of the second and third Sephiroth, Wisdom and Understanding, the I and H of IHVH, the Supernal Father and Mother.

[3] As the mediating path between them.

CHAPTER XXIX

Concerning the Hair of Microprosopus

570. WE have learned that from the skull of His head (*i.e.*, *of Microprosopus*) hang one thousand times a thousand myriad myriads of locks of black hair, and they are intertwined together each to the other, and they are mingled together.

571. But there is no classification made of the locks of hair separately, because pure and impure alike adhere to each other therein, and here (*the description above given*) mentions both pure and impure together.

572. In all those sides which are pure, and in all those which are impure, there are intricate and dense locks of hair, some of which are soft, some hard.

573. And in single locks doth the hair hang down, curls upon curls, which emit flames, and hang down in beautiful and strong array, like those of a brave hero victorious in war.

574. They are excellent as the great and foliated cedars. This is that which is written, Cant. v, 15: "Excellent as the cedars."

575. The curling locks are parted on this side and on that above the head.

576. Also we have learned that they remain in curls because they proceed from many fountains of the three canals of the brain.

577. For from the fountain of one cavity of the skull proceedeth the hair, and it becomes curls upon curls (*formed*), from the fountains proceeding from that cavity.

578. From the second cavity there go forth fifty fountains, and from those fountains the hair issueth, and it becometh curls upon curls, and they are mingled with the other locks.

579. From the third cavity there go forth a thousand times a thousand conclaves and assemblies, and from them all the hair issueth; and it becometh curls upon curls, and they are mingled with the other locks.

580. And therefore are those locks so curling, and all the progeny of them is produced from the three cavities of the brain of the skull.

581. And all those curls hang down and are spread over the sides of the ears.

582. And therefore is it written, Dan. ix, 18: "Incline thine ear, O my God, and hear."

583. And in those curls there are found alike right and left,[1] light and dark, mercy and judgment, and everything (*that hath in itself the qualities of*) right and left dependeth thence (*from Microprosopus*), and not from the Ancient One.[2]

584. In the parting of the hair appeareth a certain slender path, which hath a certain connection with that path of the Ancient of Days, and from that path are divided six hundred and thirteen paths,[3] which are distributed among the paths of the precepts of the law.

585. Like as it is written, Ps. xxv, 6: "All the paths of the Lord are mercy and truth unto such as keep His covenant and His testimony."

586. We have learned that in the single locks a thousand

---

[1] Whereas Macroprosopus is symbolized only by the right side of the profile.

[2] For the reason I have given in the preceding note.

[3] The precepts of the law are said to be 613 in number, which is also expressed by Gematria in the words "Moses our Rabbi"; MShH RBINV, *Mosheh Rabbino* = 40 + 300 + 5 + 200 + 10 + 50 + 6 = 613.

times a thousand utterances of the speech of the Lord are found, which depend from the single locks.

587. Among them some are hard (*rigorous*) and some soft (*merciful*), as (*belonging unto*) the Lord of the equilibrium (or, the Lord of mercy, who is an equilibrium between these); and therefore is He (*Microprosopus*) said to include right and left.

CHAPTER XXX

CONCERNING THE FOREHEAD OF MICROPROSOPUS

588. THE forehead of the skull is the inspection of inspection, and it is not uncovered, except in that time when it is necessary to visit sinners for the purpose of examining their deeds.

589. Also we have learned that when that forehead is uncovered, all the lords of judgment are stirred up, and the whole universe is brought under judgment.

590. Save in that time when the prayers of the Israelites ascend before the Ancient of Days, and entreat mercy for His children; then is uncovered the forehead of the benevolence of benevolences,[1] and it shineth down upon this (*forehead*) of Microprosopus, and judgment is quieted.

591. Over this forehead there goeth forth a certain portion of hair, which is extended over it from the brain, which produceth the fifty gates (*of understanding*).

592. And when it is expanded, that brow glows with anger; it is the inspector of the sinners of the world—namely, of those who are shameless in their deeds.

593. Like as it is written, Jer. iii, 3: "And thou hadst the forehead of a woman who is a whore, thou refusedst to be ashamed."

594. And we have learned that that hair subsisteth not in that part of the forehead; so that it may be uncovered against those who remain steadfast in their iniquities.

595. And when the Holy One—blessed be He!—is awak-

---

[1] Namely, that of Macroprosopus.

ened, that He may be pleased with the just, the Countenance of the Ancient of Days shineth upon the Countenance of Microprosopus, and His forehead (*that of Macroprosopus*) is uncovered, and illuminateth that forehead (that of Macroprosopus), and then is called the time of benevolence.

596. But as often as judgment threateneth, and that forehead of Microprosopus is uncovered, there is uncovered the forehead of the Ancient of the Ancient Ones, and judgment is mitigated and is not exercised.

597. We have learned that that forehead is expanded into two hundred thousand rednesses of rednesses, which are contained therein, and are included therein.

598. And when the forehead of Microprosopus is uncovered, licence is given unto all those to destroy. But when the forehead of the benevolence of benevolences is uncovered, so that it may shine upon that forehead (*of Microprosopus*) and upon all those (*rednesses*), then are they quieted.

599. Also we have learned by tradition: Twenty-four superior judgments are found, and they are all called *Netzachim*, or Victories; howsoever, while (*in the arrangement of letters, NTzCHIM, the singular*) *Netzach* is called Victory (*i.e., means that*), the neighboring letters[2] (*M and N in NTzCHIM*), being permuted, (*we obtain MTzCHIN, singular*) *Metzach* (*meaning*) forehead.

600. Therefore (*the same word signifieth*) forehead and Victory, which is in the plural victories. And this is that which is given by tradition: The Victory of victories. And they are in the forehead, but certain among them are extended in the body in (*certain*) known parts.

601. This is the exotic tradition: What is that which is written, 1 Sam. xv, 29: "Also the Netzach of Israel doth not lie nor repent, for He is not man that He should repent."

---

[2] *I.e.*, in their usual place in the order of the alphabet.

602. Now have we declared that Arcanum according to its constitution. All that Victory which is expanded in the body, at that time when the world is to be judged and converted, admitteth repentance, neither executeth judgment if they be converted.

603. For what reason? Because the matter resteth in that place which is called Adam, and He may repent.

604. But if that Victory be seen and uncovered in that part of the head just spoken of—namely, the forehead—there is neither time nor opportunity for repentance.

605. Wherefore? Because it is not that place which is called Adam, for the countenance and the nose are not uncovered, but the forehead alone.

606. And in that part—(*i.e.*, *the forehead*) the whole countenance is not found, for that (*forehead*) is not called Adam, and therefore is it said: "He is not a man that He may repent" (*i.e.*, *He, HOAVA, H, is not Adam*). *So* also is it as regardeth the (*proportion of*) Victory in the other parts of the body (*of Macroprosopus*).

CHAPTER XXXI

CONCERNING THE EYES OF MICROPROSOPUS

607. THE eyes of the head (*of Microprosopus*) are diverse from all other eyes. There is a shadowy darkness cast by the eyebrows which is (*as if it were*) painted above the eyes, whence all eyes are overshadowed with a dark shade.

608. Curling hairs hang down from the curls of the hair which is above them, and mark the form of the eyebrows above the eyes, at the commencement of the forehead.

609. And in both (*the eyebrows*) are contained seven hundred times a thousand lords of inspection who reside above the eyelids.

610. In the eyelids radiate one thousand four hundred myriads (*of hairs*), which adhere to the edges and form the eyelashes; and far above these is the inspection of the eye of the Ancient of Days.[1]

611. And as often as those eyelids (*of Microprosopus*) are raised, the same eye (*i.e., that of Macroprosopus*) appeareth, just as when the eyes of any man are opened when he awaketh from sleep.

612. And (*the eyes of Microprosopus*) behold the open eye (*of Macroprosopus shining down upon them*), and they are rendered brilliant with a certain brilliant whiteness of the good

---

[1] True to all the previous symbolism, the eye of the Ancient of Days, Macroprosopus, is here spoken of, instead of eyes in the plural number, seeing that, as I have before remarked, he is rather to be symbolized by a profile than by a full face.

eye (*i.e., that of Macroprosopus, because in Him "all is right"*—
i.e., good—and there is no left).

613. Like as it is written, Cant. v. 12: "Washed with milk."
What is "with milk"? With this excellent primal whiteness.

614. And in that time is there found with Him (*i.e., Microprosopus*) an intuition of mercy, and therefore the prayer of
the Israelites ascendeth, because His eyes are opened (*i.e.,
those of Microprosopus*), and are whitened with that whiteness (*of the eye of Macroprosopus*).

615. Like as it is written, Ps. xliv, 23: "Awake; why sleepest Thou, O Lord? Arise."

616. And truly as often as His eyes are not open, all the
lords of judgment subdue the Israelites, and the other nations have dominion over them.

617. But whensoever He openeth His eyes, these are illuminated from the good eye (*of Macroprosopus*), and mercy is
over Israel; and His eye turneth around and executeth vengeance upon the other nations.

618. This is that same which is written, Ps. xxxv, 23:
"Awake, and arise." "Awake!" and (*Thine eye*) shall be illuminated with that whiteness. "Arise!" so that it may exercise judgement upon those who have overcome them.

619. When his eyes are opened they appear beautiful as
those of doves; in color, white, red, and black, and golden
yellow.

620. And this eye (*otherwise, this whiteness*) is not uncovered except when it is looked upon by the good eye, and
then all those colors are covered (otherwise, bathed) with
this whiteness of the rays.

621. From those colors, when they are uncovered, go forth
seven eyes of Providence, which issue from the black of the
eye.

622. This is that which is said, Zach. iii, 9: "Upon one stone
seven eyes."

623. What is the "one stone"? The black of the eye.

624. From the red go forth seven emissaries, who deflect toward the left side, and they flame with fire, which is toward the north side, and they are combined, so that they may be expanded into the world for the purpose of uncovering the ways of sinners.

625. This is that which is written, Zach. iv, 10: "Those seven are the eyes of the Lord going forth throughout the whole earth."

626. From the yellow go forth seven pure splendors (otherwise lights), which are turned toward the south side, and they are combined so that they may be extended into the world, toward those ways which are necessary to be uncovered (otherwise toward those deeds, etc.).

627. Like as it is written, Job xxxiv, 21: "Because His eyes are upon the ways of man." And when they are illuminated with that whiteness, then they behold all the lords of truth, in order to do good unto the world because of them; and every glance (*of those eyes*) is benevolent toward Israel.

628. But with the red color He beholded those who are bound; which is intimated in these words, Exod. iii, 7: "In seeing have I seen"; "In seeing," for the purpose of doing good unto them; "I have seen," that by vindicating them I may deliver them from their afflictors.

629. And therefore is it written, Ps. xliv, 24: "Awake: wherefore sleepest Thou, O Lord? Arise! forsake us not for ever." "Awake and arise." There are two inspections, two openings, two good things; there is mercy, there is also vengeance.

630. The first color is red, hidden and inclosed within red; in comparison with it, all other reds do not seem to be (*red*).[2]

---

[2] Meaning that it is so brilliant that all other red colors seem poor and pale in comparison with it.

631. Around this red goeth a certain black thread (*of color*), and surroundeth it.

632. This second color is black, like that stone which goeth forth from the abyss once in a thousand years into the great sea.

633. And when that stone[3] goeth forth there cometh a tempest and a storm upon the great sea,[4] and its waters are troubled, and (*their motion soundeth as*) a voice, and they are heard by the great fish which is called Leviathan.

634. And this stone goeth forth, and is whirled onward in the current of the sea, and goeth forth thence; and this is so great a blackness[5] that beside it all other blacknesses are as nought (otherwise, now it is withdrawn because all the other paths are hidden and enshrouded by it).

635. And such is the blackness of the black (*part of*) the eye, which includeth and concealeth all the remaining blacknesses; and about that blackness there is found a certain red thread (of color) which surroundeth that blackness.

636. The third color is the yellow of all yellows, which includeth and concealeth all other yellows, and in the circumference of that yellow there whirl around two threads (*of color*), a red thread on the one direction, and a black thread in another direction; and they surround that yellow color.

637. But when that white brilliance whirleth around it, and the eye flameth with that white brilliance, all those other colors are not at rest, and are submerged in the lowest depths thereof; the red, the yellow, and the black are not

---

[3] Cf. Rev. viii, 8. This also suggests alchemical symbolism.

[4] The great sea is Binah, and the great fish is Leviathan, "whose head is broken by the waters of the great sea." ("Book of Concealed Mystery," i. § 28; Ps. lxxiv, 13; and Rev. xiii.)

[5] Cf. the "blackest of the black" of Hermes Trismegistus.

seen, only that white brilliance alone; which receiveth its light from Him, even from the Ancient of Days.

638. And from that (*white brilliance*) all the inferiors shine, neither is any color seen save that white brilliance alone. And therefore are all the lords of redness and blackness, which are as it were twin (*colors*), displaced.

639. This is the same which is written, Cant. iv, 2: "Which go up from the washing, which are all twins."

640. What is this, "From the washing"? From that white brilliance of the excellent holy eye; for all are twins, the one (*color*) is as the other.[6]

641. But truly doth not he (the author of the Canticles) say that the teeth are each in turn like a shorn flock; and thou sayest that all these are twins?

642. Nevertheless, the sense is that this whiteness of them is as that whiteness of the eyes (*of Microprosopus*) when they are made brilliant by the white brilliance of the supernal eye (*of Macroprosopus*).

643. And the just are about to understand and behold that thing in the Spirit of Wisdom.

644. Like as it is written, Isa. lii, 3: "Because they shall see eye to eye." When? "When the Lord shall bring again Zion."

645. Also it is written, Num. xiv, 14: "By whom Thou, O Lord! art seen eye to eye":[7] and then the opening of the eyes is toward good.

646. For there is an opening of the eyes toward good, and there is also another (*opening of the eyes*) toward evil.

647. Toward good, like as it is written, Dan. ix, 18: "Open

---

[6] *I.e.*, the black and the red, which are here represented as simultaneously involving each other.

[7] In our version it is translated "face to face," and not "eye to eye"; but in the original Hebrew it is *Ayin Be-Ayin*, "eye to eye."

Thine eyes and behold our desolations, and the city over which Thy name hath been pronounced." Here it is toward good.

648. But toward evil, like as it is written, Isa. xxxiii, 20: "Thine eyes shall see Jerusalem a quiet habitation, a tabernacle that shall not be taken down; not one of the stakes thereof shall ever be removed." Here truly it is toward good and toward evil, because the one existeth not without the other.

649. We have learned it in the "Book of Concealed Mystery." What is this? "Thine eyes shall see Jerusalem a quiet habitation." Is not Jerusalem therefore a quiet habitation? Also it is written, Isa. 1, 21: "Justice dwelt therein." But in the place wherein justice is found there is not rest, neither is it at peace (otherwise: In the place wherein judgment dwelleth and is found, this justice is not rest, etc.).

650. For verily this is the true interpretation: "Thine eyes shall see Jerusalem a quiet habitation" (is thus to be explained). The habitation is said to be quiet, in respect of the Ancient of Days, who looketh upon those eyes (*of Microprosopus*).

651. For truly His eye is quiet and tranquil; the eye of mercy the eye which altereth not from this aspect unto any other aspect.

652. And therefore is it written OINK[8] (*instead of* OINIK) "They shall behold Thine eye:" not Thine eyes, (*seeing* OINK *is written*) without the second I, *Yod*.

653. But how cometh it that it is said Jerusalem, and not Zion? It is properly thus said for the purpose of subjugating judgment which was found therein, and for exciting mercy upon it.

654. Also have we learned this. It is written, Deut. xi, 12:

---

[8] OINK signifies "thine eye," in the singular.

"The eyes of the Lord thy God are upon it, from the beginning of the year even unto the end of the year." This is that which is written: "Justice dwelt therein"; because therein are found many most severe judgments, as in all other instances.

655. But in the time to come there shall be found therein one eye of mercy (*namely*) the eye of the Ancient of Days.

656. This is that which is intimated, Isa. liv, 7: "But with great mercies will I gather thee."

657. Where, because it is said "with mercies," what is (*the meaning of the adjective*) "great" (*used herewith*): Assuredly because mercy is duplicated, (*namely*) the mercy of the Ancient of Days (*Macroprosopus*), which is called "great mercies."

658. And the mercy of Microprosopus, which is called mercies plain and unqualified, seeing that in Him there are right and left,[9] (*symbolizing the balance of*) Justice and Mercy. And therefore is it said: "And in great mercies will I gather thee"; those, namely, of the Ancient of Days.

659. This have we learned. In those eyes (*of Microprosopus*), and in the two colors of them—namely, in the red and in the black—there are said to abide two tears, and when He, even the Holy of the Holy Ones, desireth to have mercy upon the Israelites, then He sendeth down those two tears so that they may grow sweet in the (*waters of the*) great sea.

660. The great sea, which is that of excellent wisdom, so that in that stream (otherwise, white brilliance) and in that fountain they may be cleansed; and they go forth from the great sea, and there is mercy upon the Israelites.

---

[9] Right and left exist in Microprosopus, while in Macroprosopus all is right. The latter is rather to be symbolized by a profile, as I have before remarked, than by a full face, as in the case of the former.

CHAPTER XXXII

CONCERNING THE NOSE OF MICROPROSOPUS

661. WE have learned it in the "Book of Concealed Mystery." The nose of Microprosopus. From the nose is the countenance known. In this nose is diverse symbolism.

662. For it is written, Ps. xviii, 8: "There went up a smoke out of His nose,[1] and fire out of His mouth devoured; coals were kindled by it."

663. "There went up a smoke out of His nose." In this smoke are included both the fire and the burning coals; for there is no smoke without fire, neither fire without smoke. Truly all things result (*herefrom:* otherwise, are kindled *herein*) and go forth from His nose.

664. Also we have learned that when these three things are associated together which are included in that smoke which issueth from the nose, the nose[2] is lengthened.

665. And therein are two colors, for the smoke bloweth and rusheth forth black and red; and they call it *Aph*,[3] wrath; and *Chimah*, fervor; and *Meshachith*, perdition.

666. And if thou sayest wrath and fervor, it is well, since

---

[1] The ordinary English version renders it "nostrils" and not "nose," but in the Hebrew the word is singular.

[2] Isa. xlviii, 9 is translated in the ordinary English version: "For my name's sake will I defer mine anger"; but Parkhurst in his Hebrew and Chaldee Lexicon, art. CHTH, says the correct rendering is "for my name's sake will I lengthen my nose." Knorr von Rosenroth, in his Latin version of § 664, renders it by "corrugatur," which is hardly correct.

[3] The word *Aph*, stands alike for the words "nose" and "anger."

it is written, Deut. ix, 19: "Since I have feared because of wrath and fervor." For these are the black and red smoke. But whence is added *Meshachith*, perdition?

667. Because it is written, Gen. xiii, 10: "Before that the Lord destroyed Sodom and Gomorrah." But the word, *Shachith*, denoted perdition brought about by burning, kindled fire.

668. Also we have learned that there are five⁴ *Geboran*, severities in this conformation of Microprosopus, and they ascend in one thousand and four hundred severities, GBVRAN; and they are extended in His nose, and in His mouth, and in His arms, and in His hands, and in His fingers.

669. And therefore is it written, Ps. cvi, 2: "Who can declare the *Geburoth*, powers of the Lord?"

670. Hence it is written, "powers," Geburoth (*in the plural number*); and it is written, 1 Chron. xxix, 11: "Thine! O Lord, are Gedulah and Geburah,"⁵ in the singular (*number*).

671. Assuredly thus have we learned. When all those severities are amalgamated into one, then are they called one Geburah.

672. And all those powers, Geboran, commence to de-

---

⁴ If we carefully examine this obscure passage, I think we shall find that the number five is the key to unlock its symbolism; for five is the fifth Sephira, *Geburah*, Strength or Severity, which operates through Judgment, and ultimately through the numbers and intelligences of the planet Mars. Now, the 1,400 severities are the fivefold form of RP, *Raph*, which = the idea of terror, and RP = 280, which x 5 = 1,400. And the least number of 1,400 is 1 + 4 + 0 + 0 = 5. Also 1,400 = ATh = chaos, or substance of anything. Finally, these are extended into five parts of Macroprosopus—*viz.*, nose, mouth, arms, hands, fingers. And the number 5 = H.

⁵ See Introduction. GBVR (the root being GBR) = 211 = IAR, a flood. This is of course by Gematria.

scend from the nose. And from it depend a thousand times a thousand and four hundred myriads in their single (*forms*).[6]

673. And from that smoke which issueth from his nose depend a thousand times a thousand myriads, and four hundred and five which belong to this (*idea of*) Severity.[7] For all the severities depend from this nose.

674. For it is written, Ps. cxlv, 4: "From generation unto generation shall they praise thy works, and announce thy *Geburoth*."

675. And when that *Geburah*, Strength, commenceth (*to be manifested*), all the severities radiate thence. and are sharpened, until they descend in the form of a swift-whirling fire-flaming sword (Gen. iii, 24.)

676. It is written, Gen. xix, 13: "For we will destroy this place." Also it is written, Gen. xiii, 10: "Before that the Lord destroyed Sodom and Gomorrah." And again, Gen. xix, 24: "The Lord rained upon Sodom and Gomorrah."

677. Assuredly thus have we learned: There is no judge over the wicked, but they themselves convert the measure of Mercy into a measure of Judgment.

678. But how do they convert it thus? Also it is written, Mal. iii, 6: "I, the Lord, change not."

679. Assuredly as many times as the Ancient of the Ancient Ones and that White Head uncovereth the benevolence of benevolences, great mercies are found everywhere.

680. But when that is not uncovered, all the judgments of Microprosopus are prepared; and in this manner, if it be

[6] This formidable sounding arrangement is only our previous 1,400, considered on another plane of operation, in the material world.

[7] This is 1,400 again in its most material forms in Asiah; the number five at the end is simply the number of the Sephira of Severity added to the other.

permitted us to say so, Mercy becometh Judgment; that is, the most Ancient One of all.

681. We have learned in Barietha:[8] "When the Ancient of the Ancient Ones uncovereth the benevolence of benevolences, all those lights which are called by a similar name shine, and Mercy is found in all things.

682. But when that Concealed One of the Concealed Ones is not uncovered, and those lights shine not, judgments are stirred up, and Judgment is exercised.

683. Who therefore is the cause of that Judgment? The benevolence of the benevolences, because it is not uncovered, and therefore do sinners change Mercy into Judgment (*as regardeth themselves*).

684. But because this is said, Gen. xix, 24: "From the Lord out of heaven," it is said concerning Zauir Anpin, Microprosopus.

685. And whence is this obtained? Because it is written (*in the preceding passage*): Men Ha-Shamayim, out of heaven. (*But the word Ha-Shamayim, is equivalent to*) Ash Ve-Mim,[9] fire and water, Mercy and Judgment, in the antithesis of that (*condition*) wherein no Judgment is found at all.

686. We have learned that this nose (*of Microprosopus*) is short,[10] and when the smoke commenceth to issue therefrom, it departeth thence swiftly, and Judgment is exercised.

687. But what hindereth that nose that it may not pro-

[8] See *ante*, § 388 of this book.

[9] In the *Sepher Yetzirah*, to which work I have already had occasion to refer more than once, the letter SH is said to symbolize fire, and therefore SHMIM may be said to be fire and water.

[10] In contradistinction to that of Macroprosopus, who is called also Arikh Aphim, Long of Nose, as well as Arikh Anpin, Vast of Countenance.

duce smoke? The nose of the Ancient and Holy One; for He is also called before all others *Arikh Aphim*, Long of Nose.

688. And this is the Arcanum which we have learned: Between the two words, IHVH, IHVH, the Lord, the Lord, an accent is interpolated[11] (*whensoever these two are found in juxtaposition in Scripture*).

689. For wheresoever any name is repeated twice over, a distinction is made (*between them*), as when it is said, Gen. xxii, 11, "Abraham, Abraham"; also, Gen. xlvi, 2, "Jacob, Jacob"; also, 1 Sam. iii, 10, "Samuel, Samuel"; where, by the *Psiq* accent, these pairs of names are distinguished; excepting that place, Exod. iii, 4, "Moses, Moses," where no accent interveneth.

690. For what reason? "Abraham, Abraham," Gen. xxii, 11 (*herein therefore is an accent introduced because that*) the latter (*of these two names*) denoteth that which is perfect, but the former that which is not as yet perfect; for at this time he is perfected with ten temptations, and therefore is the (*Psiq*) accent interpolated, for at this time he can hardly be said to be the same man as he was before.

691. (*When it is said*) "Jacob, Jacob" (Gen. xlvi, 2), the latter denoteth that which is perfect, the former that which is not as yet perfect; for now the messenger had come to him from his son Joseph, and over him was the Schechinah at rest.

692. Also, now at this time was perfected in the earth the

---

[11] This accent is called *Psiq*, and in the grammar of Gesenius is classed as the twentieth accent, or the fifth of the third series known as the "lesser distinctives." It is represented by a vertical line placed between the two words to which it applies. An example of its use is to be found in Exod. xxxiv, 6: "The Lord, the Lord (*between these two words a Psiq accent is introduced*), merciful and gracious, long suffering and abundant in goodness and truth." It is worthy of note that the word here translated "long-suffering" is *Arikh Aphim*, Long of Nose.

holy tree, similar unto the Supernal One, in having twelve limitations and seventy branches,[12] which were not hitherto completed; and therefore the latter denoteth that which is perfect, and the former that which is not as yet perfect; whence the accent falleth between them.

693. In the passage, "Samuel, Samuel" (1 Sam. iii, 10), an accent is also interpolated: wherefore? The latter name denoteth that which is perfect; the former that which is not as yet perfect; for now he is a prophet, whereas before this he was not as yet a prophet.

694. But when it is said, Exod. iii, 4: "Moses, Moses," no accent is interpolated, because he was perfect from the very day of his birth, seeing it is written, Exod. ii, 2: "And she saw him, that he was good."

695. So also here between these two names of the Lord, Exod. xxxiv, 6, the *Psiq* accent is interpolated; for the first is indeed a perfect name, but the latter is thoroughly and completely perfect.

696. But Moses speaketh thus in the place of Judgment, in order that for them he may cause Mercy to descend upon Microprosopus from the Most Holy Ancient One.

697. For thus is the tradition. So great was the virtue of Moses that he could make the measures of Mercy descend.

698. And when the Ancient One is uncovered toward Microprosopus all things are beheld in the light of Mercy, and the nose is appeased, and fire and smoke issue not therefrom.

699. Like as it is written, Isa. xlviii, 9: "And with my praise will I defer mine anger for thee."

---

[12] That is, the *Autz Chaiim*, or tree of life, composed of the Sephiroth and the Schemahamphorasch, the former being ten and the latter seventy-two. The twelve limitations are the twelve sons of Jacob, and the seventy branches the total number of the combined families.

700. Also we have learned: The nose hath two nostrils. From the one issueth a flaming smoke, and it entereth into the opening of the Great Abyss.

701. And from the other nostril issueth a fire which is kindled by its flame; and it floweth into four thousand worlds, which are upon His left side.

702. Truly, he who is the cause of war is called the fire of the Lord, the consuming fire, the fire which consumeth all other fires.

703. And that fire is not mitigated save by the fire of the altar.

704. And that smoke which issueth forth from the other nostril is not mitigated unless by the smoke of the sacrifice of the altar. But all things depend from the nose.

705. Therefore is it written, Gen. viii, 12: "And the Lord smelled a sweet savor." For all these are attributed unto the nose, to smell a savor, and to emit smoke and fire, and red color, and therefore is it opposed unto the benevolence (*namely, the forehead*).

706. And for that cause is it written, Exod. iv, 14: "And the anger of the Lord was kindled." Deut. vii, 4: "And the anger of the Lord will be kindled." Exod. xxii, 24: "And My wrath is kindled." Deut. vi, 15: "Lest the wrath of the Lord be kindled." Which are all to be understood concerning Zauir Anpin, or Microprosopus.

CHAPTER XXXIII

CONCERNING THE EARS OF MICROPROSOPUS

707. THIS have we learned. It is written, 2 Kings xix, 16: "Incline, O God, Thine ear and hear"; namely, that ear which is hidden beneath the hair, and the hair hangeth down over it, and yet the ear is there for the purpose of hearing.

708. And from the inner part of the ear, elaborated with strongly marked concave formations, like a winding spiral ladder, with incurvation on every side.

709. But wherefore with curvings? So that He may hear both good and evil.

710. Also we have learned: From that curving part within the ears depend all those Lords of Wings concerning whom it is written, Eccles. x, 20: "For a bird of the air shall carry the voice, and the Lord of the Wings shall tell the matter."

711. Within that ear, (*the Spirit*) floweth from the three hollow places of the brain into this opening of the ears. And from that afflux (*the Spirit*) the voice departeth into that profound depth (otherwise, incurvation) and is conjoined with (*the Spirit*) in that distillation, as well good as evil.

712. In good: as it is written, Ps. lxix, 33: "For the Lord heareth the poor." In evil; as it is written, Num. xi, 1: "And the Lord heard, and His wrath arose, and the fire of the Lord was kindled against them."

713. And that ear is closed from without, and a depth (otherwise an incurvation) proceedeth within that gallery of inspiration from the brain.

714. So that the voice may be collected together within, neither issue forth thence, and that it may be guarded and shut in on every side; hence it is in the nature of an Arcanum.[1]

715. Woe unto Him who discloseth secrets! For he who revealeth secrets doth the same thing as if he should deny the superior formation, which is so arranged that the secrets may be collected together, and that they may not issue forth without.

716. Also we have learned in Barietha[2]: At that time when they call aloud in their troubles, and the hairs are moved from before the ears, the voice entereth into the ears through that channel, and the spirit of distillation from the brain (*entereth into that channel likewise*).

717. And in the brain is it collected (otherwise, and it slideth on into the brain), and departeth through the nostrils of the nose, and is bound, and the nose becometh shorter (*that of Microprosopus, namely*) and groweth with fire, and fire and smoke issue forth; and from those nostrils are excited all the severities, and vengeance is exercised.

718. Truly before that from those nostrils the fire and smoke issue forth, that voice ascendeth upward, and slideth into the beginning of the brain; and the two tears flow down from the eyes.

719. And by means of that voice the smoke goeth forth, and the fire from the brightness which openeth those gates; for through that voice which entereth into the ears all these things are excited and urged forth (otherwise, are mingled together).

720. And therefore is it written, Num. xi, 1: "And the Lord heard, and His wrath was kindled, and the fire of the

[1] Because in a similar manner a secret is guarded and shut in.
[2] See *ante*, § 388. Barietha is "Traditio extra urbem."

Lord was kindled against them." For through that hearing of that voice the whole brain is stirred up.

721. We have learned. It is written, 2 Kings xix, 16: "Incline, O my God, Thine ear"; like as if it should be said, "Let six hundred thousand myriads of those wings which depend from those ears be elongated"; and they are all called the ears of the Lord.

722. When therefore it is said, "Incline, O Lord, Thine ear," (this phrase) "Thine ear," is that of Microprosopus.

723. From one cavity of the brain do those ears depend; and from the fifty gates[3] which proceed from that cavity, this is one gate, which extendeth and goeth forth and openeth into that channel of the ear.

724. Like as it is written, Job xxxiv, 3: "Because the ear trieth words." Also it is written, Ps. vii, 10: "And He trieth the heart and reins."

725. And in proportion to the expansion of that cavity of fifty gates which proceedeth into the body, so is the latter expanded even in that place wherein the heart resideth.

726. Therefore concerning the ear it is said that in it is made probation; and also concerning the heart it is said that in it is made probation; because that they proceed (alike) from one place.

727. We have learned in the "Book of Concealed Mystery" that, like as this ear proveth as well the good as the evil, so all things which are in Microprosopus have part good and part evil, right and left, Mercy and Judgment.

728. And this ear is contiguous unto the brain; and because it is contiguous unto the brain, hence that voice is directed into a cavity which entereth into the ear.

729. Therefore concerning the ear it is called hearing; but

[3] This refers to the "fifty gates of the Understanding"—alluding to the third Sephira.

in this hearing, Binah, the Understanding (*the third Sephira*) is comprehended; for, also, to hear, is the same as to understand, because that thereby all examinations are examined together.

730. And those words of the Lord of Lords are given forth so that they may be heard, so that they may be meditated upon and be understood.

731. Come, behold! it is written, Hab. iii, 1: "O Lord! I have heard Thy voice, and was afraid."

732. This passage hath this meaning: When that holy prophet heard and understood and knew, and was occupied with those conformations, it is written: "I was afraid." Rightly was it (*so written*) that he should be afraid and be broken before Him, for these words are said concerning Microprosopus.

733. When further he understood and knew, what is then written? "O Lord! revive Thy work in the midst of the years." But concerning the Ancient of Days is this said.

734. And in every passage wherein is found the Lord, the Lord, with Yod He twice, or with Aleph Daleth and Yod He, the one belongeth unto Microprosopus, and the other unto the Ancient of the Ancient Ones. For because all these things are one certain thing, hence by one name are they called.

735. Also we have learned. When is the full name expressed? When it is written, *the Lord Elohim.* For that is the full name of the Most Ancient of all, and of Microprosopus; and when joined together they are called the full name. But other forms are not called the full name, like as we have established.

736. When it is said, Gen. ii, 8: "And the Lord Elohim planted," etc., the name is given in full, where the discourse is concerning the planting of the garden; and whensoever the Lord Elohim occurreth the full name is expressed.

737. In IHVH IHVH all things generally are comprehended, and then mercies are stirred up over all things.

738. (*When it is said*) "O Lord! revive Thy work in the
midst of the years," concerning the Ancient of Days is it
said.

739. What is "Thy work"? Zauir Anpin, Microprosopus.

740. "In the midst of years." These are the former years,
which are called *Yemi Qedem*, former days; and not years,
Olahm, or of the world.

741. The former years are the former days; the years of
the world are the days of the world.[4]

742. And here (*it is said*): "In the midst of the years." What
years? The former years.

743. "Revive it." Concerning whom is it said, "Revive
it"? Concerning Microprosopus. For all His splendor is
preserved by those years, and therefore is it said, "Revive
it."

744. "In wrath remember mercy." He looketh to that supernal benignity wherein mercies are excited over all; (*those
mercies*) who desire compassion, and to whom mercy is
owing.

745. We have learned, Rabbi Schimeon said: "I call to witness the heavens which are above me, toward all those who
stand around, that great joy ariseth in all the worlds because of these words.

746. "Also these words excite joy in my heart; and in the
veil of excellent expansion are they hidden and do they ascend; and He, the Most Ancient One of all, preserveth them,
He, the Concealed and Hidden of all.

747. "And when we began to speak my companions

---

[4] In connection with § 741, note Ps. lxxvii, 5: "CHSHBTHI IMIM MQDM
SHNVTH OVLMIM, I have considered the days of old, the years of ancient
times."

knew not that all these words therein were worthy hereof in any degree.

748. "O how blessed is your portion, companions of this conclave! and blessed is my portion with you in this world, and in the world to come!"

CHAPTER XXXIV

CONCERNING THE BEARD OF MICROPROSOPUS

749. RABBI SCHIMEON commenced and said, Deut. iv, 4: "And ye shall cleave unto the Lord your God," etc.

750. What nation is so holy as Israel? for it is written concerning them, Deut. xxxiii, 29: "Blessed art thou, O Israel![1] who is like unto thee?" Because that they are applied unto God in this world through the holy name.

751. And in the world to come more than here, for therein shall we never be separated from that conclave wherein the just are assembled.

752. And this is that which is written: "And ye shall cleave *in* the Lord"; for it is not written *"Chedebeqim Le Tetra-grammaton*, Ye shall cleave *unto* the Lord"; but *"Be the Lord, in* the Lord," properly.

753. We have learned this. There is a descent from the beard which is venerable, holy, excellent, hidden and concealed in all (*the beard, namely, of Macroprosopus*), through the holy magnificent oil, into the beard of Microprosopus.

754. And if thou shalt say that this beard is not to be found, for that even Solomon only spake of the cheeks,[2] but not at all of the beard.

755. Truly thus have we learned (*we make answer*) in the "Book of Concealed Mystery." It is that which is hidden and recondite, and of which mention is not made, neither is it

---

[1] It must not be forgotten that Israel is a mystical name which was substituted for Jacob.

[2] Namely, in the description in the Song of Solomon, ch. v.

uncovered; it is that which is venerable and excellent before all things, seeing that it is concealed and hidden.

756. And since the beard is the praise and perfection and dignity of the whole countenance, in these sacred things it is found to be hidden, neither is it discerned.

757. And that beard is the perfection and beauty of the countenance in Microprosopus. In nine conformations is it disposed.

758. But when the venerable beard of the Ancient of the Ancient Ones shineth upon this beard of Microprosopus, then the thirteen fountains of excellent oil flow down upon this beard.

759. And therein are found twenty-two parts, and thence extend the twenty-two letters of the holy law.

760. Also we have learned that this beard departeth from His ears, and descendeth and ascendeth, and toucheth upon the places of fragrance.

761. What are the places of fragrance? Like as it is said, Cant. v, 13: "Like a bed (*singular*) of spices," and not "beds" (*plural*).

762. But this beard of Microprosopus is disposed in nine conformations.

763. And also the hairs being black, and in careful order, like a handsome man, as it is written, Cant. v, 15: "Excellent as the cedars."

764. The first conformation. The hair is conformed from the portion which is above, and there goeth forth therefrom a spark which is of most intense brilliance; and it goeth forth from the Absolute of the pure ether, and passeth beneath the hair of the head, even beneath those locks which are above the ears; and it descendeth in front of the opening of the ears, hair above hair, even unto the beginning of the mouth.

765. The second conformation. The hair goeth forth, and

ascendeth from the one part of the mouth even unto the other part of the opening of the mouth; and it descendeth beneath the mouth unto the other side, hair above hair, in beautiful arrangement.

766. The third conformation. From the midst, beneath the nose, and beneath the two nostrils, there goeth forth a certain path, and short and coarse hairs fill up that path; and the remaining hairs fill up the place from this side unto that, around this path.

767. But this path is not clearly seen (*to be continued*) below (*the mouth*), but only the upper part of it which descendeth even unto the beginning of the lips, and there is this path applied.

768. The fourth conformation. The hair goeth forth and is disposed in order, and ascendeth, and is spread over His cheeks, which are the place of fragrance of the Ancient One.

769. The fifth conformation. The hair is wanting, and there are seen two apples on this side and on that, red as a red rose, and they radiate into two hundred and seventy worlds, which are enkindled thereby.

770. The sixth conformation. The hair goeth forth as in a tress about (*the border of*) the beard, and hangeth down even unto the commencement of the vital organs, but it descendeth not unto the parts about the heart.

771. The seventh conformation. That the hairs do not hang over the mouth, but that the mouth is uncovered on every side, and that the hairs are disposed in order about it.

772. The eighth conformation. That the hairs descend beneath the beard, and cover the throat, so that it cannot be seen; all those hairs are slender, hairs above hairs, plentiful in every part.

773. The ninth conformation. That the hairs are mingled together with those which are joined unto them; and that they all are in equality from the cheeks even unto those

hairs which hang down; all are in fair equality, like a brave man, and like a hero victorious in war.

774. Through these nine conformations there proceed and flow down nine fountains of magnificent oil, and these indeed flow down from that magnificent supernal oil (*of the beard of Macroprosopus*) into all those inferiors.

775. Those nine conformations are found in form herein (otherwise, in this beard); and in the perfection of the conformation of this beard is the inferior son of man called the brave man.[3]

776. For whosoever seeth (*in sleep*) that his beard existeth in proper form,[4] in him is found courage and strength.

777. Rabbi Schimeon spake unto Rabbi Eleazar, his son, and said: "Arise, O my Son, and expound the parts of the holy beard in its conformations."

778. Rabbi Eleazar arose, and commenced and said, Ps. cxviii, 5: " 'I called upon *Yah*, in my distress; *Yah* heard me at large. The Lord is on my side, I will not fear; what can man do unto me? The Lord taketh my part with them that help me, and I shall see my desire upon mine enemies. It is better to trust in the Lord than to put any confidence in man; it is better to trust in the Lord than to put any confidence in princes.'

779. "Herein are delineated the nine conformations of this beard. For King David had need of these dispositions, that he might vanquish other kings and other nations.

780. "Come, behold! After that he had said these nine conformations, he added (verse 10): 'All nations compassed me about, but in the name of the Lord I will destroy them.'

781. "Therefore did he rehearse those conformations

---

[3] Meaning, that as is the Supernal Man so is the earthly man.

[4] Meaning, if he dreams that his beard is arranged like that of Microprosopus.

which we have repeated. But what was the necessity for so doing? Because that he said: 'All nations compassed me about.' For in this disposition of those nine conformations which are the name of the Lord, are they cut off from the earth.

782. "This is that same which is written: 'In the name of IHVH will I destroy them.'

783. "Also this have we learned in the 'Book of Concealed Mystery.' David hath here enumerated the nine conformations; of which six consist in the holy name, for there are six names;[5] and there are three in the word *Adam*, or man.

784. "And if thou shalt say that there are only two (*in the word Adam*), assuredly there are three, because also the princes pertain unto the idea of the word Adam.[6]

785. "This have we learned. These are the six names, because it is thus written: 'I called upon Yah in my distress.' The first.

786. " 'Yah heard me at large.' The second.

787. " 'The Lord is on my side, I will not fear.' The third.

788. " 'The Lord taketh my part with them that help me.' The fourth.

789. " 'It is better to trust in the Lord.' The fifth.

790. " 'It is better to trust in the Lord.' The sixth.

791. "But in the word *Adam*, Man, are three; for it is written: 'The Lord is on my side, I will not fear; what can *Adam*, Man, do unto me?' The first.

792. " 'It is better to trust in the Lord than to put any confidence in princes.' The second.

793. " 'It is better to trust in the Lord than to put any confidence in *Adam*, Man.' The third.

---

[5] *I.e.*, there are six repetitions of the name of the Deity in the verses under consideration.

[6] Meaning, that the word princes, in the verse "than to put any confidence in princes," refers also to man.

794. "And come, behold! There is an Arcanum hidden in this thing; and wheresoever in this passage mention is made of the word *Adam*, thereunto the Holy name is joined; and truly for a reason, seeing that man subsisteth only through that which is analogous unto himself.

795. "But what is it which is analogous unto him? The Holy Name; because it is written, Gen. ii, 7: 'And *Tetragrammaton Elohim* created *Adam, Man,*' with the full Name, which is IHVH ALHIM, analogous to him (*Adam*), seeing that IHVH, the Lord, denoteth the masculine, and ALHIM, *Elohim,* the feminine.[7]

796. "And therefore in this passage there is no mention made of *Adam,* Man, without the Holy Name.

797. "Also we have learned this. It is written: 'I called upon *Yah,* in my distress; *Yah,* heard me at large.' IH is here twice repeated, IH, IH, in reference to the two jaws unto which the hairs (*of the beard*) adhere, and from which it is seen that the hairs issue and depend.

798. "He hasteneth and saith (*i.e., King David*): 'The Lord, is on my side; I will not fear; IHVH taketh my part with them that help me; wherein the Name is not written defectively (*IH as before, but IHVH*) which is the Holy Name, and with this Name mention is also made of man.'

799. "And what is this thing which is said, 'What can *Adam,* Man, do unto me?' It is thus, as we have learned by tradition: All those sacred diadems of the King,[8] when He is conformed in his dispositions (*that is, when the letters of the*

---

[7] For Elohim is from the *feminine* root ALH, and is really a FEMININE PLURAL, for while many masculines form their plurals in VTH, many feminines conversely form theirs in IM. In both these cases, however, the gender of the singular is retained in the plural. (See Gesenius' Hebrew Grammar, § 86, art. 4.)

[8] The King—*i.e.*, Microprosopus.

Lord are all conjoined together), are called *Adam*, Man, which is the Form[9] which comprehendeth all things.

800. "But when any portion is taken away therefrom (*that is to say, when it is said IH, and not IHVH*), then is understood (*Microprosopus*) the Holy Name (*by the letter I, Yod*) and *Tauara*, or the Gate (*that is, the Bride, to whom is attributed the name Adonai, whose number when written in its plenitude is 671,*[10] *as the word* THORA *or* THROA *exhibiteth it, summed up in the letter H, He, of the name IH*), and that which is therein.

801. "When therefore it is called the Lord, man is mentioned, with the Gate Tauara included, and those which are therein [otherwise, concerning the inferior worlds. And when it is taken away from the gate (*that is, when the letters Vau and He are not joined hereunto, of which the latter denoteth the inferior gate*), then is understood the Holy Name (*by the Yod*), and the Gate and those which are therein (by *the He in the name IH*). But when it is called IHVH, it is called the man, ADM, and all the rest (*conjoined therewith*), namely, the gate and those (*paths*) which are therein.].[11]

802. "And therefore did David enumerate those nine conformations; because he unto whom it is allowed to touch the beard of the King can do all which he desireth.

803. "Wherefore then the beard, and not the body?

[9] For it is said that the Lord, written thus in the Hebrew letters, gives the figure of a man. For *Yod* = the head, *He* = the arms, *Vau* = the body, and *He* final = the legs. (See Table of Hebrew letters in Introduction.)

I
H
V
H

[10] That is to say, when the letters of ADIN are spelt thus: ALP, DLTH, NVN, IVD, *Aleph, Daleth, Nun, Yod;* for A + L + P + D + L + TH + N + V + N + I + V + D = 1 + 30 + 80 + 4 + 30 + 400 + 50 + 6 + 50 + 10 + 6 + 4 = 671. And THORA or THROA = 400 + 70 + 200 + 1 = 671 also.

[11] The long piece above in brackets, but in ordinary type, is from the Cremona Codex.

Because the body is hidden behind the beard, but the beard hath no place (*of concealment*) behind the body.

804. "But he in reckoning it proceedeth in a duplex manner [12]—once as we have given it; and next thus, when he saith: 'I called upon Yah in my distress.' The first.

805. " 'Yah heard me at large.' The second.

806. " 'The Lord is on my side; I will not fear.' The third.

807. " 'What can man do unto me?' The fourth.

808. " 'The Lord taketh my part with them that help me.' The fifth.

809. " 'And I shall see my desire upon mine enemies.' The sixth.

810. " 'It is better to trust in the Lord.' The seventh.

811. " 'Than to put any confidence in man.' The eighth.

812. " 'It is better to trust in the Lord.' The ninth.

813. " 'Than to put any confidence in princes.' The tenth.[13] (Otherwise: 'It is better to trust in the Lord than to put any confidence in man.' The seventh. 'It is better to trust in the Lord.' The eighth. 'Than to put any confidence in princes.' The ninth.)

814. " 'I called upon Yah in my distress.' What is this which he saith? Assuredly doth David say all these things which are here said concerning the form of the beard."

815. Rabbi Yehudah answered and said: " 'I called upon Yah in my distress.' From the part where the beard beginneth to extend, which is from the more remote part (*is one*), before the ears, beneath the hair (*is the second*). And therefore is it twice said, IH, IH.

[12] Referring to the order of the conformations, and the way in which in the passage those referring to IHVH and ADM are conjoined.

[13] The reader will of course also observe that these answer to the ten Sephiroth.

816. "But in that place wherein the beard is expanded, and descendeth before the ears, in wider extension, the name of *Adam*, Man, hath place (that is to say, the complete Lord). Also this expansion was necessary to David when he wished to subject to himself the kings and nations through the dignity of this beard. (Otherwise, when therefore he saith, 'The Lord is on my side, I will not fear;' for this is such a one who spareth not the wicked, and this was altogether necessary, etc.)

817. "Also we have learned this in the 'Book of Concealed Mystery':[14] Whosoever seeth in his sleep that he toucheth the beard or mustache of the supernal man with his hand, or extendeth his hand unto it, let him know that he is at peace with the supernals, and that those who afflict him are about to be subjected unto him."[15]

818. "We have learned that the supernal beard is disposed in nine conformations, and that it is the beard of Microprosopus."

[14] See *ante*, "Book of Concealed Mystery," ch. iii. § 17.
[15] This is apparently the end of Rabbi Yehudah's short interpolation regarding the duplicated IH. Rabbi Eleazar now apparently resumes the discourse.

CHAPTER XXXV

CONCERNING THE FIRST PART OF THE BEARD OF MICROPROSOPUS

819. "IN the first conformation the hair is disposed from above, and goeth forth before the opening of the ears, beneath the locks which hang down over the ears; and the hairs descend, hairs above hairs, even unto the beginning of the mouth.

820. "This have we learned. All those hairs which are in the beard are harder than all the hairs of the locks of the hair of the head. But the hair of the head is longer and bendeth more easily, while these hairs (*of the beard*) are not so long.

821. "Of the hairs of the head some are hard and some are soft.

822. "And whensoever the white locks of the Ancient of Days reach forward into Microprosopus, it is written that, Prov. i, 20: 'Wisdom crieth without.'

823. "What is this (*word*) 'without'? In this (*instance*) in Microprosopus, wherein are conjoined the two (*forms of the*) brain. Two forms of the brain, sayest thou? But it should rather be said, four forms of the brain.

824. (*Assuredly*) "there are three (*forms of the*) brain in Microprosopus, and they are found in the three cavities of the skull of His head.

825. "And there is one calm and tranquil brain residing in its own clear brilliancy, which comprehendeth all the three (*forms of the*) brain, and from it are brought forth the productions of the hairs which are produced and continued in

equilibrium in the white hair into that part of Micro-prosopus, into His three (forms of) brain (*namely*), *so* that therein in Him are found four (*forms of the*) brain.

826. "And hence are perfected the four texts which are written on the phylacteries, because in them is contained the Holy Name of the Ancient of Days, the Ancient of the Ancient Ones, and that of Microprosopus.

827. "For this is the perfection of the Holy Name, concerning which it is written, Deut. xxviii, 10: 'And all the people of the earth shall see that the name of the Lord has been invoked over thee, and they shall be afraid of thee.'

828. "The Name of the Lord is this very Name of the Lord, which formeth the canals and hollows of the phylacteries.

829. "And therefore is it said: 'Wisdom crieth without,' Prov. i, 20, because it is herein found (*i.e., in Microprosopus*).

830. "For truly the Ancient of the Ancient Ones, even He who is concealed with all concealments, is not found, neither doth His wisdom come forth (*openly*); seeing that His wisdom is concealed in *all*, and doth not make itself manifest.

831. "And since there are four (*forms of the*) brain associated together, and that herefrom, even from Microprosopus, there flow down four fountains in four directions, and that they are all distributed from one fountain, which proceedeth from them all, therefore are there four.[1]

---

[1] This four proceeding from one, and containing all things, is precisely the Pythagorean doctrine of the Tetractys, which Pythagoras probably obtained from qabalistic sources, though indeed most religions of antiquity attached considerable importance to this number four. Four is said to contain the whole Decad, because the sum of the first four numbers = ten; 1 + 2 + 3 + 4 = 10. But eight is the reflection of four, and eight is IHVH ADNI. And 1 + 2 + 3 + 4 + 5 + 6 + 7 + 8 = 36, the number of the Decans (or groups of ten degrees) in the Zodiac. But 5 + 6 + 7 + 8 = 26, the number of the

832. "Also we have learned: From the Wisdom which is comprehended in the Quaternary the hairs flow down, which hang in curls upon curls, and all are strong and close, and they extend and flow down singly each in its own direction.

833. "And so many thousand thousand myriads of myriads depend from them that they are innumerable.

834. "This is that same which is written, Cant. v, 11: 'His locks are bushy, *Teltelim*,' as if it were THLI THLIM, curls heaped upon curls.

835. "And all are strong and close (*fit*) for breaking (*whatsoever is opposed to them*), hard as the rock, and as hardest stone.

836. "Until they can make openings in the skull, and the fountains can flow down beneath the locks, those strong fountains flow forth in separate directions, and in separate ways.

837. "And because those locks are black and obscure, it is written, Job xii, 22: 'He discovereth deep things out of darkness, and bringeth out to light the shadow of death.'

838. "Also we have learned that those hairs of the beard are so much harder than those hairs of the head, because these alone make themselves so prominent, and are easily found, and are hard in their paths.

839. "Wherefore sayest thou that they are hard? Is it because they all symbolize Judgment? By no means; for truly in those dispositions Mercy as well as Judgment is found.

840. "When the thirteen fountains of the rivers of oil descend, all these are mercies.

841. "But yet we have learned that all those hairs of the

IHVH. Therefore thirty-six represents the sum of the letters of the Lord, and the number of the Sephiroth.

beard are hard. Wherefore? Those which symbolize mercies necessarily must be hard in order to divert the course of Judgment.

842. "And all those which denote Judgment, are also firm; and therefore it is necessary in every instance that they should both be hard.

843. "When the Universe hath need of Mercy, mercies are strong, and prevail over Judgment; but when it requireth Judgment, Judgment is strong, and prevaileth over Mercy; and therefore is it necessary that in each instance they should be firm and strong.

844. "And whensoever Mercy is required, those hairs which symbolize Mercy stand forth, and the beard is evident in those hairs only (otherwise, is contained by those hairs only), and all are abundant mercies.

845. "But when Judgment is required the beard is evident in those hairs only (*which denote judgment*), and all consist in judgments.

846. "But when that holy white beard[2] is uncovered, all these (*hairs denoting Mercy*) and all those (hairs denoting Judgment) are alike illuminated and made brilliant, like as when a man cleanseth himself in a deep river from his uncleanness.

847. "And all consist together in Mercy, and there is no Judgment to be found at all.

848. "And when all those[3] nine forms shine together, all are made white with Mercy.

849. "And therefore Moses saith in another place, Num. xiv, 18: 'The Lord is *Arikh Aphim*, long-suffering (*literally long of nose*), and of great mercy.'

[2] Which is of course that of Macroprosopus, the Ancient of Days.

[3] The nine conformations into which the beard of Microprosopus is divided.

850. "And that which he had said concerning truth,[4] Exod. xxxiv, 6, he addeth not (*in this passage*), because the Arcanum of the matter is these nine measurements which shine down from the Ancient of Days into Microprosopus.

851. "For when Moses in the second passage rehearseth these praises of God, Num. xxiv, 18, he enumereth the nine conformations; and these are the conformations of the beard, even those which are found in Microprosopus, and descend from the Ancient of Days and shine down into Him.

852. "The word AMTH, *Emeth*, Truth, therefore dependeth from the Ancient One; whence in this passage Moses saith not: 'And in truth.'

853. "We have learned that the hairs of the head of Microprosopus are all hard and curling, and not soft.[5]

854. "For we see that in Him three forms of the brain are found in the three cavities (*of the skull*), which shine forth from the hidden and concealed brain.

855. "And because the brain of the Ancient of Days is tranquil and quiet, like good wine upon the lees, hence all His hairs are soft, and anointed with excellent oil.

---

[4] I give these two passages side by side for the reader's benefit.

Exod. xxxiv, 6 and 7: "The LORD, the LORD GOD, merciful and gracious, long-suffering, and abundant in goodness and truth.

"Keeping mercy for thousands, forgiving iniquity and transgression and sin, and that will by no means clear the guilty; visiting the iniquity of the fathers upon the children, and upon the children's children, unto the third and to the fourth generation."

Num. xiv, 18: "The LORD is long-suffering, and of great mercy, forgiving iniquity and transgression, and by no means clearing the guilty, visiting the iniquity of the fathers upon the children unto the third and fourth generation."

[5] It appears to read thus in the Chaldee and in the Latin alike, though this statement is contradicted distinctly both in § 587 and in § 857. I should

856. "And therefore is it written, Dan. vii, 9: 'His head like pure wool.'

857. "But those which are in Microprosopus are partly hard, and partly not hard, because they all hang down, and are not diverted from their course.

858. "And therefore Wisdom[6] floweth forth and proceedeth (therefrom); but it is not the Wisdom of Wisdom, for that is quiet and tranquil.

859. "For we have learned that no one knoweth the brain of the Ancient of Days save Himself alone.

860. "This is that very thing which is said, Job xxviii, 23: 'God understandeth the way thereof,' etc.; which (words) are spoken concerning Microprosopus."

861. Rabbi Schimeon said (unto him): "Blessed be thou, O my son! in that Holy and Blessed One, in this world and in the world to come!"

---

think the word "LA, not," before "soft," is a mistake, or else that the passage refers to the hair of the beard, and not that of the head.

[6] That is, Chokmah of the second Sephira, and not that Chokmah which is its root concealed in Kether; for in Kether are all the other Sephiroth contained.

CHAPTER XXXVI

CONCERNING THE SECOND PART OF THE BEARD OF MICROPROSOPUS

862. "THE second conformation. The hair goeth forth and ascendeth from the beginning of (*the one side of*) the mouth even unto the beginning of the other side of the mouth; and descendeth beneath the mouth unto the other side, hair above hair, in beautiful arrangement. Arise, Rabbi Abba!"

863. Rabbi Abba arose, and commenced and said: "When the disposition of this beard is instituted in the formation of the King, then is He Himself like a brave hero, strong and beautiful in appearance, valiant and conquering.

864. "This is that same which is written, Ps. cxlvii, 5: 'Great is our Lord and great is His power.'

865. "And whilest He is mitigated by the disposition of the venerable and holy beard (*of Macroprosopus*), and this (*beard of Microprosopus*) reflected that, then through its light is He called 'God merciful,' Exod. xxxiv, 6: 'and gracious, long-suffering, and abundant in goodness and in truth.' And thus is the second disposition instituted.

866. "When He shineth in the light of the Ancient of Days, then is He called 'abundant in Mercy,' and when another of the other forms is considered, in that form is He called 'and in truth,' for this is the light of His countenance."

CHAPTER XXXVII

CONCERNING THE THIRD PART OF THE
BEARD OF MICROPROSOPUS

867. "ALSO we have learned. Bearing iniquity is this second conformation called, like as in the Holy Ancient One.

868. "But because that path which goeth forth in the third disposition beneath the two nostrils is filled with short and rigid hairs; hence because of that path these conformations are not called 'bearing iniquity and passing over transgression'; but these are collected together in another place.

869. "Also we have learned in Barietha that three hundred and seventy-five mercies are comprehended in the benignity of the Ancient of Days; which are all called primal benignities.

870. "Like as it is said, Psalm lxxxix, 50: 'Where are thy former mercies?' and they are all comprehended in the benignity of the Most Holy Ancient One, the most concealed of all.

871. "But the benignity of Microprosopus is called *Chesed Olahm*, the benignity of time.

872. "And in the 'Book of Concealed Mystery' (*have we learned*) that on account of the former benignity of the Ancient of Days is he called 'Abundant in Benignity.' But in Microprosopus (*the word*) 'mercy' is placed alone and absolutely.

873. "And therefore is it here written: 'And abundant in benignity'; and again it is written: 'Keeping mercy for thousands'; plain and without addition.

874. "And now we have taught concerning this Name, 'And abundant in benignity,' because therefrom is mitigated the (*interior*) benignity, so that it may shine into all the lights (otherwise, this Name, 'Abundant in mercy,' stretcheth down even unto the 'mercy' which is so called absolutely, so that it may illuminate it, and kindle the lights).

875. "For we have learned that that path which descendeth beneath the two nostrils of the nose is filled with short hairs; and concerning this path, that it is written: 'Passing over transgression' (otherwise, and the shorter hairs fill that path. But that path is not called 'Passing over transgression'); because there is therein no occasion for passing over; for a double reason.

876. "Firstly, because that path is a hard place for passing over. (Otherwise, because the hairs which are found therein are hard.)

877. "Secondly, because the passing over of that path descendeth even unto the commencement of the mouth.

878. "But concerning this it is written, Cant. v, 13: 'His lips like roses[1] (that is, red as roses), dropping sweet-smelling myrrh while passing over'; which denoteth notable redness.

879. "And this path of that place is a duplex form, and is not mitigated, whence he who wisheth to threaten toucheth that path twice with his hand."

---

[1] The English version of this passage renders it, "His lips like lilies, dropping sweet-smelling myrrh." The word here translated roses by Knorr von Rosenroth is *Shoshanim*, which I think should undoubtedly be translated "lilies," as in the ordinary version. The symbology of this chapter is very difficult and obscure.

CHAPTER XXXVIII

880. "THE fourth conformation. This path of hairs is disposed, and ascendeth and descendeth in His cheeks into the place of fragrance.

881. "This disposition is fair and beautiful in appearance, and it is Glory and Honor; and it is taught in Barietha that the Supernal Honor, *Hod*, goeth forth and is crowned, and floweth down, so that it may be comprehended in His cheeks, and is called the Honor of the Beard.

882. "And thence depend Glory and Honor, which are as vestments, and as very precious purple, so that He may be clothed therewith.

883. "For it is written, Ps. civ, 1: 'Thou art clothed with Honor and Majesty.' (Otherwise: In the fourth conformation the hair goeth forth, and is disposed, and ascendeth and descendeth in the cheeks, in the places of fragrance. This conformation is elegant and beautiful in appearance, and it is the supernal glory. And this is the tradition: The supernal glory goeth forth, and is crowned, and floweth down in the beauty of the cheeks. And this glory is called the glory of the beard; and from it depend honor and glory, the vestments of adornment, those magnificent purple garments wherewith he is clothed. Concerning which it is written: 'Thou art clothed with honor and majesty, which are the forms of clothing. In this form of man is he formed, rather than in any other form.')

884. "These are the dispositions denoting the clothing (*of the divine form*), and he is more fitly symbolized under this figure of man than under any other forms.

885. "Also we have learned, that when this glory (*of Microprosopus*) is illuminated by the light of the excellent beard,[1] and emitteth light into the other dispositions, then it is called 'Bearing Iniquity' on the one side, and 'Passing over Transgression' on the other side.

886. "And therefore in Scripture is it called by the name of his jawbones.

887. "And in the 'Book of Concealed Mystery' is the same called Glory, *Hod*,[2] and Honor, *Hadar*, and *Tiphereth*,[3] Beauty.

888. "And unto *Tiphereth*, Beauty, appertaineth the title 'Passing over Transgression,' since it is said, Prov. xix, 15: 'And it is His Beauty (*Tiphereth*) to pass over transgression.'

889. "Also we have learned that we should only refer that *Tiphereth*, Beauty, unto the ninth conformation (*of the beard of Microprosopus*); as it is said, Prov. xx, 29: 'And the beauty of young men is their strength.' And therefore also is it (the ninth conformation) called Beauty; and when they are weighed together in the balance they are as one."

890. Rabbi Schimeon said unto him: "Worthy art thou, O Rabbi Abba! for which reason mayest thou be blessed by the Most Holy Ancient One, from whom all blessings proceed.

891. "The fifth conformation. The hair is wanting, and there appear two apples, on this side and on that, red as red roses, and they radiate into two hundred and seventy worlds.

892. "As to those two apples, when they shine on either

---

[1] Namely, that of Macroprosopus.
[2] The eighth Sephira.
[3] The sixth Sephira.

side, from the light of the two supernal apples (*the cheeks of Macroprosopus*), redness is removed therefrom, and a white brilliance cometh upon them.

893. "Concerning this is it written, Num. vi, 25: 'the Lord make His face shine upon thee, and be gracious unto thee.' Seeing that when they shine he is blessed by the world.

894. "But when that redness is stirred up (*in them*), it is written, *ibid.* 26: 'the Lord take away His wrath from thee'; as if it were said: 'It is taken away, and wrath is no longer found in the world.'

895. "We have learned that all the lights which shine from the Most Holy Ancient One are called the former benignities, because all those lights are the benignities of time."

896. "The sixth conformation. The hair goeth forth as it were in a certain tress, among the hairs in the circumference of the beard; and this is called one of the five angles which depend from the *Chesed*, Mercy and Compassion.

897. "And it is not permitted to lose this benignity, as it is said.

898. "Therefore is it written, Lev. xix, 27: 'Thou shalt not lose the angle of any beard.'

899. "The seventh conformation is that the hairs hang not over the mouth, and that the mouth is uncovered on every side. Arise thou, Rabbi Yehudah."

900. Rabbi Yehudah arose, and commenced, and said, Dan. iv, 17: " 'This matter is by the decree of the Watchers.'

901. "Many thousands of myriads stand around, and are preserved by this mouth, and depend therefrom, and all those are called (*by the general title of*) the mouth.

902. "As it is written, Ps. xxxiii, 6: 'And all the host of them by the Spirit of His mouth.'

903. "And by this Spirit which goeth forth from the mouth are all those exteriors clothed who depend from that mouth.

904. "And by that mouth, when that path is opened, are clothed many true prophets; and they are all called the mouth of the Lord.

905. "And in that place where the Spirit goeth forth no other thing is mingled therewith; for all things wait upon that mouth, that they may be clothed with the Spirit going forth therefrom.

906. "And this disposition ruleth over the six (*foregoing conformations*), because herein are all things established and comprehended.

907. "And therefore are the hairs (*of this conformation*) equal around the mouth, and this itself is uncovered on every side."

908. Rabbi Schimeon said (*unto him*): "Blessed be thou, by the Most Holy Ancient One.

909. "The eighth conformation is that the hairs descend beneath the beard, covering the throat, that it cannot be seen.

910. "For we have learned in the exotic tradition that neither the throat nor any of its parts (*are apparent*) through (*the hair*). And if in the time of contest (otherwise of Victory, *Netzach*[4]), during such contest any portion of (*the throat*) be visible, then it appeareth like Strength (*Geburah*).[5]

911. "For we have learned that a thousand worlds are contained thereby.

912. "This is that which is said, Cant. iv, 4: 'Wherein there hang a thousand bucklers, all shields of mighty men.' And this 'thousand shields' is an Arcanum.

913. "It is related in the 'Book of Concealed Mystery' that 'all the shields of the mighty men,' which come from the

[4] The seventh Sephira.
[5] The fifth Sephira.

side of the rigours,[6] are derived from those severities (*Geboran*).

914. "The ninth conformation is that the hairs flow down in perfect equilibrium even unto those hairs which hang down beneath, and all of them in beautiful arrangement, like (*that of*) a brave hero, (*of*) a chief victorious in war.

915. "Because all the hairs follow those which hang down, and all are joined unto those which hang down, and each holdeth its own course.

916. "Concerning this it is written, Prov. xx, 29: 'The beauty of a young man is his strength.'

917. "And He appeareth upon the (*Red*) Sea,[7] like a beautiful youth, which is written in Cant. v, 16: 'Excellent (or young) as the cedars.'

918. "Like a hero hath He exhibited His valor, and this is that *Tiphereth, Chila, Ve Geburatha, Ve Rechemi*, Beauty, Strength, and Valor, and Mercy."

[6] We must not forget that in Microprosopus are "right and left," Mercy and Justice.

[7] Microprosopus, the *Vau*, V, of IHVH. The sea is Binah, the Supernal Mother, the third Sephira, and the first H of IHVH.

CHAPTER XXXIX

CONCERNING THE BODY OF MICROPROSOPUS IN GENERAL, UNDER THE CONDITION OF AN ANDROGYN

919. THIS have we learned. Rabbi Schimeon said: All those dispositions and all those words ought to be revealed by those who are weighed in the balance, and not by those who have not entered therein, but by those who have both entered therein and departed therefrom. For he who entereth therein and goeth not out therefrom, better were it for that man that he had never been born.

920. The sum of all is this: The Ancient of the Ancient Ones existeth in Microprosopus; He is the all-existent One; He was all, He is all, He will be all; He will not be changed, neither is He changed, neither hath He been changed.

921. But by means of those conformations hath He conformed Himself in that form which comprehendeth all forms, in that form which comprehendeth all names.

922. But this form wherein He Himself only appeareth is in the similitude of this form; and is not that form, but is analogous unto this form[1]—namely, when there are associ-

[1] I take the sense of this second clause to be that He is not really in the outward and visible form of a material man; but that he can be best expressed hereby in a symbolic spiritual form. Cf. Ezek. i, 26: "And upon the LIKENESS of the throne was the LIKENESS as the APPEARANCE of a man above it."

ated therewith the crowns and the diadems and the perfection of all things.

923. And therefore is the form of the man the form of the superiors and inferiors which are included therein.

924. And because that form comprehendeth the superiors and the inferiors, therefore by such a disposition is the Most Holy Ancient One conformed; and thus also is Microprosopus configurated in this disposition.

925. And if thou sayest: What, then, is the difference between the one and the other?

926. Assuredly all things are equally (*balanced in the*) Unity. But yet from our point of view (*i.e., from our plane*) His paths are divided, and from our point of view (*on our plane*) is judgment found, and from the side which is turned toward us are (*His attributes*) by turns duplicated.[2]

927. And these Arcana are not revealed save unto the reapers of the Sacred Land.[3]

928. For it is written, Ps. xxv, 14: "The secret of the Lord is with them that fear Him."

929. Also it is written, Gen. ii, 7: "*Va-Yeyetzer Tetragrammaton Elohim Ath Ha-Adam.*"[4] And the Lord Elohim formed the substance of man, completed (*him*) formation by formation from the most ethereal (*portion*) of the refined (*element of*) earth (otherwise formation within formation from the best, etc.).

930. And this is *Va-Yeyetzer* VIITzR, (written with two *Yods*, I's *instead of* VITzR, *Va-Yetzer, with one Yod,* I).

931. Wherefore? There is an Arcanum of the Most Holy Ancient One, and an Arcanum of Microprosopus.

---

2 In connection with this section read ch. i, §§ 5, 6, 7, and 8, of the "Book of Concealed Mystery."

3 *I.e.*, to the students of the Qabalah.

4 See also "Book of Concealed Mystery," ch. ii, § 23.

932. VIITzR, *Va-Yeyetzer*, and formed. What did (*the Lord Elohim*) form? Form in form. And this is VIITzR.

933. And what is form in form? The two names, which are called the full name, *the Lord Elohim.*

934. And this is the Arcanum of the two I's, *Yods,* in VIITzR; and of how it hath been conformed form within form; namely, in the disposition of the perfect name, the Lord Elohim.

935. And in what are they comprehended? In the supernal beard (otherwise, in this supernal form which is called (*the supernal*) man; the man who comprehendeth Male and Female equally).

936. And therefore is it written: "*Ath Ha-Adam* (τὸν ἄνθρωπον), the substance of man," because it comprehendeth equally the Male and the Female, for to the word ADM, ATH is subjoined, so as to extend and exaggerate the species which is here produced. Most assuredly here therefore is it as Male and as Female.

937. "*Ophir Men Ha-Adamah,* from the rust of the ground," dust, form within form (otherwise, from the most ethereal portion of the refined element of earth, one within the other).

938. But wherefore are all these things so? Because that from the supernals there was sent down into him (*Man*) the Arcanum of the supernal Arcana, even the end of all Arcana.

939. This is that which is herein written: "*Ve-Yepech Be-Ephaiu Neschamath Chiim,*" and breathed into his nostrils the Neschamath[5] of (*their*) lives.

940. Their souls, from which all things living, superiors

---

[5] Neschamath is either the plural of Neschamah, *defectively written,* or else shows that Neschamah is *in regimine* to Chiim, and evidently means the united higher souls of *both Adam and Eve conjoined in one body.*

and inferiors, alike depend, and wherein they have their existence.

941. *"Va-Yehi Ha-Adam Le-Nephesch Chiah,* and the Adam
was formed into a living Nephesch," so that it (*the physical
Nephesch form*) might be attached to himself (otherwise, so
that it might be developed in him), and that he might form
himself into similar conformations;[6] and that he might pro-
ject himself in that Neschamah from path into path,[7] even
unto the end and completion of all the paths.

942. So that in all this Neschamah might be found, and
that it might be extended into all, and that it itself might be
still one.

943. Whence he who taketh this away from the universe
doth the same thing as if he should take away this
Neschamah for the purpose of setting in its place another
Neschamah beside it.[8]

944. And therefore shall such a man and his remem-
brance be cut off from generations unto generations.

[6] That is, into conformations similar to those of the Supernal Man.

[7] That is, into forms, conditions, and qualities analogous to the
Sephiroth.

[8] Apparently the sense of this passage is intended to combat Atheism,
and to show that it is logically absurd to deny the existence of a Spirit of
God which works in the universe; inasmuch that if this be denied, at all
events something analogous in its general properties will have to be substituted for it.

CHAPTER XL

945. THUS in this Adam androgyneity hath commenced to be disposed when it hath been formed in its disposition. It hath commenced from His back. (Otherwise, from His breast.)

946. Between the two arms, in that part whereunto the beard hangeth down, which is called Tiphereth, the Beauty.

947. And this Beauty is expanded and disposeth two breasts.

948. And it is separated from the back, and produceth the Head of a Woman completely covered on every side by Her hair as far as to (*the limits of*) the face of Her head.

949. Insomuch that through that Tiphereth, Beauty, Adam becometh in one body, Male and Female.

950. This is that which is written, Isa. xliv, 13: "According to the beauty of a man, *Ke-Tiphereth Adam*, that it may remain in the house."

951. When the countenance of the Female Head is created, one curled lock of hair at the back of Microprosopus hangeth over the head of the Woman.

952. And all hairs red gold are produced in Her head; yet so that other colors are intermixed therewith.

953. This is that which is written, Cant. vii, 5: "The hair of Thy head like *Argaman*, purple."

954. What is Argaman? Colors intermixed with other colors.

955. This Tiphereth, Beauty, hath been extended from the heart, and penetrateth it, and passeth through unto the other side, and instituteth the formations from the Countenance of the Woman even unto Her heart; so that from the parts about the heart it taketh its rise on this side, and in the parts about the heart it terminateth on that side.

956. Moreover, this Tiphereth is extended, and it formeth the internal parts of a Man.

957. And it entereth into and disposeth therein all mercies and aspects of mercies.

958. Also we have learned that in those internal parts are comprehended six hundred thousand Lords of Mercies, and that they are called the Lords of the Internal Parts.

959. Whence it is written, Jer. xxxi, 20: "Therefore My bowels are troubled for him, I will surely have mercy upon him, saith the Lord."

960. We have learned that this Tiphereth, Beauty, embraceth Mercies and Judgment, and that Mercy is extended in the Male.

961. And it passeth over and goeth through unto (otherwise, shineth on) the other side, and formeth the internal parts of a Woman on the side of Judgment; and thus also are Her internal parts disposed.

962. We have learned that the Male hath been conformed on His side (otherwise, from His heart), in 248[1] members; of which some are within, some without; some Mercies, some Judgments.

963. All which pertain unto Judgment, cohere in

---

[1] The number of 248 = RCHM, *Rechem* = Mercy + 248; thus conveying this idea in the number.

Judgment around the hinder part, where the Woman is extended; and they coalesce and are extended round about on that side.

964. Also we have learned that five nakednesses can be revealed on that side, which are the five judgments; and these five judgments are extended into 248 paths.[2]

965. And thus have we learned: the voice in the Woman is uncovered; the hair in the Woman is uncovered; the leg[3] in the Woman is uncovered; the hand in the Woman is uncovered; the foot in the Woman is uncovered.

966. And also, furthermore, concerning these two our companions have not inquired, yet these two have more nakedness.

967. Also, we have learned in the "Book of Concealed Mystery" that the Male is extended and conformed with His parts, and there is formed in Him forma partis tegendæ puræ, et illud est membrum purum.

968. Longitudo autem membri hujus est 248 mundorum, et omnes illi pendent in orificio membri hujus quad dicitur, I, *Yod*.

---

[2] For five is H, *He*, the number of the feminine letter in the Lord, the number also of the micro- cosm or Lesser World, the symbol or sign of which is the Pentagram. The 248 paths into which the five judgments are extended are the correlates of those of mercy.

[3] This word is *Shoq*, in the original. Fuerst translates it Leg, especially the part from knee to ankle. So does Gesenius in his Lexicon; but in his large Hebrew and Chaldee Thesaurus it is, apparently by an oversight, omitted. Zanolini translates it "Armus, Crus," and adds: "In *Berachoth*, fol. 24, 'ShVQA BAShH ORVH, Crura in muliere res pudenda sunt, scilicet crura nuda. Hinc in more positum apud Judæos est, ut ipsorum mulieres, et puellæ demissis ad talos vestibus verecundiæ caussa utantur, ne viros ad libidinem excitent.'" ("Lexicon Chaldæo-Rabbinicum," art. ShVQ.)

969. Et cum detegitur Yod, orificium membri; detegitur Benignitas superna.[4]

970. And this member is the Benignity, quo nomine tamen proprie vocatur orificium membri; neither is it called Benignity until I, *Yod*, orificii membri, is uncovered.

971. And come, behold, Abraham is not called perfect in that Benignity, until I, *Yod*, of the member is uncovered; but when that is uncovered he is called perfect.[5]

972. This is that which is written: "Walk before Me and be thou perfect; really and truly perfect," Gen. xvii, 1.

973. Also it is written, Ps. xviii, 24: "I will be upright before Him, and will keep myself from the sinner."

974. Who is he concerning whom the discourse is both in the first and second instance (*in this passage*)? Assuredly, he who uncovereth that Yod; et cavet, ne Yod istud introducat in potestatem adversam; so that he may have part in the world to come, and that he may be bound together in the sheaf of life.

975. What is this, "in potestatem adversam"? Even that which is written, Mal. ii, 11: "And hath married the daughter of a strange god."

---

[4] I have thought it advisable to retain this piece in the Latin, as it will be equally intelligible in that language to the ordinary student; and it is not so well fitted for expression in English. It contains the symbolism of the *genitalia*.

[5] This apparently refers to the qabalistical symbolism of the changing of the names of Abram and Sarai into Abraham and Sarah; ABRM and ShRI into ABRHM and ShRH; ABRM = 243 is made into ABRHM = 248 by addition of the number 5, the letter H, *He*; and ShRI = 510 is made SHRH = 505 by the subtraction of five from the final I, *Yod*; 248 is the number of the members of Microprosopus, and 5 is that of the five judgments. Hence the united numbers of Abram and Sarai, 243 + 510 = 753, which number is also obtained by the addition of Abraham and Sarah, 248 + 505 = 753; so that the total numeration of the two names remains unchanged.

976. And therefore is it written: "I will be upright before Him, because he hath become perfect in the uncovering of Yod, and I will keep myself from the sinner."

977. Et dum extenditur membrum hoc, etiam extenditur latus rigoris de illis rigoribus sinistræ in fæmina.

978. Et inseritur in fæminam, in loco quodam, et signatioram facit in nuditate, seu parte maxime contegenda in toto corpore fæminino.

979. Et ille locus dicitur nuditas ab omnibus occultanda, locus scilicet pro membro illo, quod dicitur Benignitas, ut scilicet mitigetur rigor iste, qui continet quinque rigores.

980. And that Benignity comprehendeth in itself five Benignities (otherwise, and herein existeth the Benignity from the other Benignities). And Benignity is from those on the right, but Severity from those on the left.

981. And when the latter is mitigated by the former He is called man, consisting in both aspects.

982. And therefore in all the crowns (*the former state of things*) was not permanent, before that the conformations of the King[6] were prepared by the Ancient of the Ancient Ones, so that He might construct the worlds, and form (*their*) conformations, for the purpose of establishing that Woman,[7] so that She might be mitigated.

983. Until the supernal Benignity could descend, and then the conformations of the Woman became permanent, and were mitigated by this member (of Microprosopus), which is called the Benignity.

984. This is that which is written, Gen. xxxvi: "And these are the kings which reigned in the land of Edom"; which is

---

[6] Microprosopus.

[7] Malkuth, the tenth Sephira, the Kingdom, the Queen, the Bride of Microprosopus; the Isis, Rhea, Ceridwen, Hertha, etc., of other religions; Nature, the Great Mother of us all.

the place where all the judgments are found, and they are the constitutions of the Woman.

985. For it is not written, "Who were," but "Who reigned," because they were not mitigated until all were formed, and that Benignity went forth.

986. Therefore is it said, "And he died," because they were not permanent, neither was Judgment mitigated through Judgment.[8]

987. But, and if thou sayest: "That if it be thus that all are judgments, wherefore is it written, Gen. xxxvi, 37: 'And Saul of Rechoboth[9] by the waters reigned in his stead,' for this man truly doth not appear (to symbolize) a judgment?"

988. We have learned that all denote judgment, excepting one, which last remaineth.

989. But this Saul of Rechoboth by the waters is one order (otherwise, one side or aspect), an order which is expanded, and goeth forth from Rechoboth by the waters.

990. And this is Binah, wherefrom are opened the fifty gates[10] in the aspects of the world of lights and luminaries.

991. This is what is said concerning Rechoboth by the waters. And they were not all permanent. Thou shalt not say that they were abolished, but that they were not permanent in that kingdom which is from the side of the Woman.

992. Until there was excited and extended that Last One of them all concerning whom it is said: "And *Hadar* reigned after him."

[8] Compare with this the meaning of the names of the two Pillars at the entrance to King Solomon's Temple.

[9] It is not at first sight clear why Saul of Rechoboth should be taken exception to as symbolizing judgment. But if we examine the word RChVBVTh, *Rechoboth*, by Gematria, we shall find a reason. For R + CH + V + B + V + TH = 200 + 8 + 6 + 2 + 6 + 400 + 622 = BRKTh, *Berachoth*, Blessings, and also "pools of water," which is also "Rechoboth by the waters." And "the waters" are Binah, the third Sephira.

[10] *Vide ante* in the "Book of Concealed Mystery."

993. Who is Hadar? The Supernal Benignity.[11]

994. "And the name of his city was *Paau (crying aloud)*." What is Paau? Through this the man prayeth who is worthy of the Holy Spirit.

995. "And the name of his wife was *Mechetabel*," herein are they mitigated together, and his (*Hadar's*) wife is named, which is not written concerning any other of them. *Mechetabel (which bears the signification of "as if were made better by the name of Benignity, AL, EL, MCHI TB AL")* mitigation of the one by the other.

996. "The daughter of *Matred*," the elaborations, on the side of Severity: "the daughter of *Mezahab*"; that is they have been firmly contempered and intertwined together—namely *Me*, Mercury,[12] and *Zahab*, Gold, Mercy, and Judgment.

---

[11] For HDR = 213, which = CHSD OLAH DAL *Chesed Aulaeh Da-El*, the Supernal Mercy of El = 213 also. And Chesed is the fourth Sephira, which succeeds Binah the third, as Hadar succeeds Saul of Rechoboth by the waters.

[12] This partakes of alchemical symbolism—Mezahab, the philosophical Mercury.

CHAPTER XLI

CONCERNING THE SEPARATE MEMBERS OF EACH PERSONIFICATION, AND ESPECIALLY CONCERNING THE ARMS OF MICROPROSOPUS

997. HEREUNTO have adhered together both the Woman and the Man; now in Their condition are They separated in arms and limbs.

998. Of the Male, one arm is right and the other left.

999. In the first arm (otherwise in the holy arm) three members[1] (or divisions) are bound together.

1000. And the two arms are completed. And they are perfected in three members in the right arm, and in three members in the left arm.

1001. The three members of the right arm correspond to the three members of the left arm.

1002. And therefore is mention only made of the one arm. For of the arms there is only made mention of that on the right side; but in Exod. xv, 6 it is called, "Thy right hand, O the Lord!"

1003. Therefore it is said "the right hand of the Lord," with reference to the three divisions of the Patriarchs[2] who have occupied those parts.

---

[1] As in the arm there are three natural divisions, from shoulder to elbow, from elbow to wrist, and from wrist to the tips of the fingers. The word QSHRIN, here translated "members," means, properly speaking, "zones."

[2] This word in the original is *Ebahatha*, which, according to the context, may mean simply "Fathers"; or in a more emphatic sense, "Patriarchs";

1004. And if thou shalt say: "Also these are found (*symbolized*) in the three cavities of the skull."

1005. We have learned that all these three (*as to their conceptions*) are expanded through and connected with the whole body (*of Microprosopus*) through those three which are bound together in the right arm.

1006. And therefore David desired Him, and said, Ps. cx, 1: "Sit thou with those on my right hand," that he might be associated with the Patriarchs, and sit there in the perfect throne.

1007. And therefore it is written, Ps. cxviii, 22: "The stone which the builders rejected," because that he sat on the right hand.

1008. This is that which is written, Dan. xii, 13: "And thou shalt rest, and rise again in thy lot at the limit of My right hand."[3]

1009. Like as if it were said: "Even as he who is worthy of the friendship of the King is happy when the King extendeth His right hand, and placeth him at His right hand.

1010. But when He sitteth, certain members are extended as to this right hand, but the arm extendeth not the hand (otherwise, when He sitteth, also the members are not extended, and the arm is not stretched forth but remaineth still), with its three members, of which mention hath been made before.

1011. But when sinners are stirred up and spread abroad in the world, three other members are excited, which are severe judgment, and His arm is stretched forth.

---

this latter is the sense in which it is employed in this passage. The three Patriarchs are Abraham, Isaac, and Jacob, for this word Ebahatha is *not* employed to denote the twelve sons of the latter.

[3] This is usually translated "at the end of the days." This translation is simply due to a difference in the *pointing*, the words being the same in orthography—thus, IMIN.

1012. And when that arm is stretched forth, it is as it were the right hand (*also*); but it is called "the arm of the Lord": "O the Lord! Thine arm hath been stretched forth" (1 Kings viii, 42).

1013. When these three members are contained in those three, all are called the right hand, and judgment is exercised and mercy.

1014. This is that which is said, Exod. xv, 6: "Thy right hand, O the Lord, is marvelous in power; with Thy right hand, O the Lord, wilt Thou dash in pieces the enemy"; seeing that therein are stirred up the mercies.

1015. Also, we have learned that unto this right hand adhere three hundred and fifty thousand myriads (otherwise, which are called the right hand, and one hundred and eighty-five thousand myriads) from the arm, which is called the arm of the Lord.

1016. Therefore, from either side is the arm (*i.e., it is either the right arm or the left arm*), because that it is said (*to be*) on either side of Tiphereth.

1017. For it is written, Isa. lxiii, 12: "That led Moses to his right hand, by the arm of his Tiphereth."

1018. The first expression denoteth the right; but the "arm" denoteth the left; for it is written, "by the arm of his Tiphereth," one (*side*) with the other (*i.e., right and left*).

1019. Moreover, we have learned that to that which is on the left side there adhere four hundred and fifty[4] Lords of Shields, and that they adhere unto those separate fingers.

1020. And in the single fingers there are found ten thousand Lords of the Shields. Go thou then forth, and number how many of them there are in the hand.

---

[4] 450 = ThN, *than*, which is the root of Serpent or Dragon. Compare Leviathan, which is probably formed from this root.

1021. And this right hand is called the Holy Aid, which cometh forth from the right arm, from the three members (*thereof*).

1022. And although it be called the hand, yet is it Aid, since it is written, 2 Sam. iii, 12: "And behold, My Hand is with thee."

1023. And in it are contained one thousand and four myriads and five hundred and eight thousand lords, the aiders in every world,[5] who are called the supernal hand of the Lord, the inferior hand of the Lord.

1024. And although everywhere it be called the hand of the Lord, it is understood (*that sometimes*) the left hand[6] (*is intended to be spoken of*). For if they be benevolent, it is called the right hand of the Lord, and the hand is included in the arm, and is for aid, and is called the hand; and if, on the other hand, it be not so, the inferior hand of the Lord is (*to be understood*).

1025. We have learned that when the severe judgments are excited so that they may descend into the world, that then it is written, Ps. xxv, 14: "The Arcanum of the Lord is over those who fear Him."

---

[5] That is, on every qabalistical plane.

[6] For in Microprosopus there is always right and left, Mercy and Justice; while in Macroprosopus all is said to be "right." But Microprosopus is manifest, and Macroprosopus is hidden.

CHAPTER XLII

CONCERNING THE SEPARATION OF THE MASCU-
LINE AND THE FEMININE, AND CONCERNING
THEIR CONJUNCTION

1026. ALSO we have learned in the "Book of Concealed Mystery"[1] that all the judgments which arise from the Masculine are vehement in the commencement, and relax in the termination; but that those which are found to arise from the Feminine are relaxed in commencement, and vehement in termination.

1027. And were it not that they could be conjoined, the world could not suffer them; whence the Ancient of the Ancient Ones, the Concealed by all things, separateth the one from the other, and associateth them together so that at once they may be mitigated.

1028. And when He wisheth to separate them He causeth an ecstasy (*or trance*, cf. Gen. ii, 21) to fall upon Microprosopus, and separateth the Woman from His back.

1029. And He conformeth all Her conformations, and hideth Her even unto Her day, on which She is ready to be brought before the Male.

1030. This is that which is said, Gen. ii, 21: "And the Lord Elohim caused a deep sleep to fall upon Adam, and he slept."

1031. What is this, "And he slept"? This is that which is

[1] See "Book of Concealed Mystery," *ante*, ch. iii, § 27.

written, Ps. xliv, 24: "Awake! wherefore sleepest thou, O the Lord?"

1032. And He taketh away one of his sides. What is this one? This is the Woman.

1033. And She is taken away and conformed; and in Her place is inserted Mercy and Benignity.

1034. Like as it is said: "And he hath shut up flesh before her." Ezek. xxxvi, 26: "And I will take away from you the stony heart out of your flesh, and I will give you a heart of flesh."

1035. And when He wisheth to introduce the Sabbath, then did He create the spirits, and the malignant demons, and the authors of disturbance; neither at first did He finish them, until the Mother could come into Her formation, and could sit before Him.

1036. When She could sit before Him, He ceased from those creatures, and they were not completed because the Mother sat before the King, and they were associated together face to face.

1037. Who shall enter between Them? Who shall stir up war between Them mutually?

1038. Because the Arcanum of the matter is hidden in the time of the disciples of wisdom, who know our Arcanum, from Sabbath unto Sabbath.

1039. And when they are associated together, then are They mutually mitigated in that day on which all things are mitigated. And therefore are the judgments mitigated mutually and restored into order, both superiors and inferiors.

CHAPTER XLIII

CONCERNING THE JUDGMENTS

1040. ALSO, we have learned in the "Book of Concealed Mystery"[1] that when the Most Holy Ancient One desired to see whether the judgments could be mitigated, and whether these two could adhere together, that then from the side of the Woman there went forth a vehement judgment, which the world could not bear.

1041. Whence it is written: "And Adam knew Eve his wife" (Gen. iv, 1). And she conceived and brought forth *Qain*, and said: "I have acquired a man with the Lord."

1042. And She was not perfect, because She had not been mitigated, and the powerful serpent had transmitted unto Her the pollution of severe judgment; and therefore She could not be mitigated.

1043. When therefore this man Qain proceeded from the side of the Woman, he went forth rigorous and severe; severe in his judgment, rigorous in his judgment.

1044. But when he had gone forth, She Herself became thereafter weaker and more gentle. And there went forth another and gentler birth.

1045. And the former one was removed, which was so vehement and rigorous that all the judgments could not be mingled together before Her.

1046. Come and see. What is written? "And it came to pass when they were both in the field." "In the field," which

---

[1] See "Book of Concealed Mystery," ch. iii, §§ 27–31.

is known to be the supernal (*field*); "in the field," which is called the field of the apple-trees.

1047. And this judgment hath conquered his brother because he is stronger than he, and hath subdued him, and hath concealed him in his own power.

1048. Then therefore, that Holy God was stirred up regarding this—may His Name be blessed!—and took him away from the midst before him, and placed him in the mouth of the Great Abyss.

1049. And enclosed his brother by immersion in the Great Sea, so that he might temperate the supernal tears.

1050. And from them men descend in the world according to their path.

1051. And although they are concealed, yet are they extended mutually in themselves and from one body.

1052. And from that body descend the souls, NShMThHVN, of the impious, of the sinners, and of the hardened in spirit.

1053. From them both at once, dost thou think? No; but one floweth down from the one side, and another from the other.

1054. Blessed are the just, whose NShMThHVN, souls, are drawn from that Holy Body which is called Adam, which includeth all things; the place, as it were, wherein all the Crowns and Holy Diadems are associated together, arrayed in the equilibrium of balance.

1055. Blessed are the just, because all these are holy words which are sent forth through the Supernal Holy Spirit, the spirit wherein all the Holy Ones are comprehended; the spirit in whom the supernals and inferiors are collected together (otherwise, whom the supernals and inferiors hear).

1056. Blessed are ye, O Lords of Lords, Reapers of the Field, who know and contemplate those words, and know well your Lord, face to face, and eye to eye; and through those words worthy in the world to come.

1057. This is that very thing which is written, Deut. iv, 38: "Know therefore this day, and consider it in thine heart, that the Lord, *He* is Elohim, in the heavens above, and upon the earth beneath: there is none other."

1058. Where the Lord is the Ancient of Days. *Hoa Ha-Elohim*, that is the One, blessed be His Name for ever, and unto the Ages of the Ages.

CHAPTER XLIV

FURTHER REMARKS CONCERNING THE SUPERNAL MAN

1059. RABBI SCHIMEON spake, and said: Let us behold. The superiors are below, and the inferiors are above.[1]

1060. The superiors are below. That is the form of the Man which is the Universal Superior Conformation.

1061. We have learned this which is written, "And the just man is the foundation, Yesod, of the world," Prov. x, 25, because He comprehendeth the Hexad in one enumeration.[2]

1062. And this is that which is written, Cant. v, 15: "His legs are as columns, Shesh, of the Number Six."[3]

1063. We have learned in the "Book of Concealed Mystery" that in man are comprehended the Superior Crowns in general and in special; and that in man are comprehended the Inferior Crowns in special and in general.

---

[1] Which is equivalent to the great magical precept of Hermes Trismegistus in the second clause of the Smaragdine Tablet: "That which is below is like that which is above, and that which is above is like that which is below, for the performance of the miracles of the one substance."

[2] It is not at first sight clear what is meant by this statement. But if we examine the passage closely, we shall see that the "just man" is taken for Microprosopus, who is the son, the "form of the man"; "comprehending the Hexad," because he is composed of the six Sephiroth—*Chesed, Geburah, Tiphereth, Netzach, Hod,* and *Yesod.*

[3] The ordinary translation of this passage is: "His legs are as pillars of marble." SHSH may be translated either "marble" or "the Number Six," according to the pointing.

1064. The Superior Crowns in general (*are comprehended in*) the figure of all those conformations, as hath been already said.

1065. (*The Superior Crowns*) in special (*are comprehended*) in the fingers of the hands, which are *Chamesh Ke-Neged Chamesh*, Five over against (or opposed to, or chief above) Five.[4]

1066. The Inferior Crowns (*are comprehended in*) the toes of the feet, which are special and general.

1067. For the body is not seen with them, seeing they are extraneous to the body. And therefore they are not in the body, seeing the body hath receded from them.

1068. For if so, what is this, Zach. xiv, 4: "And His feet shall stand in that day?" Truly the feet of the body, the Lords of Judgments to exercise vengeance.

1069. And they are called the Lords of the Feet; and certain of them are powerful, and the Lords of the Judgments, who are below, adhere unto the inferior crowns.

1070. We have learned that all those superior conformations which are in the Holy Body, in the Male and in the Female, which (*arrangement of Male and Female*) is the proper ordering (*of the Form*) of the man, are deduced from themselves by turns, and that by turns they adhere each to its (*order of deviation*): and that by turns they flow down into themselves (*i.e., the duplicate Male and Female form*).

1071. Like as the blood floweth through the passages of the veins—now through one, now through another; now hither, now thither; from one place into another place.

---

[4] Compare *Sepher Yetzirah*, ch. i, § 3: "Ten are the restricting numerations (*Sephiroth*). The Number Ten (is that of the) fingers—Five as chief above (or over against, or opposed to) Five, CHMSH KNGD CHMSH, and the pure Unity enthroned in Her strength in the Word of Renewal, and in the Word of Might."

1072. And those interior portions of the Body bind themselves together by turns until all the worlds are illuminated, and receive benediction because of them.

1073. We have learned that all those Crowns which are not comprehended in the Body are all far distant and impure, and pollute whom they are permitted—whosoever, namely, cometh near unto them so that he may learn anything from them.

1074.[5] This have we learned. Wherefore, then, is there so great a desire for them among the Disciples of Wisdom? For no other reason than that they (*the Crowns which are impure*) should approach that Holy Body, and that thus perchance through them (*the Disciples of Wisdom*) they (the *impure Crowns*) may seek to be comprehended in that Body.

1075. But if thou sayest that if it be so, surely the Holy Angels also are not included in the comprehension of the Body.

1076. Most assuredly it is not so in the least. For if, He being absent from them, there were Holy Ones without the conformative arrangement of the Body, surely (*He being absent from them*) they could neither (*continue to*) be holy, nor to subsist.

1077. And nevertheless it is written, Dan. x, 6: "And his body like as *Tarshish*"; also, Ezek. x, 12: "And their backs full of eyes"; also, Dan. ix, 21: "The man Gabriel." All these passages refer to the analogy of the Man.

1078. Those being accepted which exist not in the ordered arrangement of the Body; for those are impure, and pollute him—namely, whosoever shall approach unto them.

---

[5] This section apparently intends to inculcate the doctrine that it is the duty of the righteous to endeavor to improve not only the ungodly but even the demons themselves.

1079. Also, we have learned that these are found to proceed from the spirit of the left side, which is not mitigated in human form; and they have gone out from the ordered arrangement of the Holy Body, neither do they adhere unto it.

1080. And therefore are they all impure, and they wander to and fro, and fly through the world.

1081. And they are entered into the mouth of the Great Abyss, so that they may adhere unto that former Judgment which had gone forth from the ordered arrangement of the Body, called the Inferior Qain.

1082. And they wander to and fro, and fly up and down, through the whole world, being carried abroad hither and thither; and they adhere not in the Syntagma of the Body.

1083. And therefore are they without, and impure, among all the hosts above and below; like as it is written, Lev. xiii, 46: "And his habitation shall be without the camp."

1084. But from the Spirit which is called Abel, which hath been more mitigated in the Syntagma of the Holy Body, others go forth who have been more mitigated, and can *adhere unto* the body, but cannot completely be *in*herent *within* it.

1085. They all hang in the air, and go forth from this genus of those Impure Ones, and hear whatsoever may be said above and below; and concerning them they have knowledge who have spoken concerning them.

1086. Also, this is the tradition in the "Book of Concealed Mystery." When the Syntagma of the Supernal Man had been mitigated as to the Holy Body, in Male and Female

---

[6] For their first conjunction produced Qain, the severe and evil judgment; their second, Abel, the milder and weaker form whom Qain absorbs; but their third produces Seth, the equilibrium of the supernals and inferiors.

form, these two were conjoined together again for the third time.[6]

1087. And the temperation of all things proceeded therefrom, and the superior and inferior worlds were mitigated.

1088. And thenceforth the superior and inferior worlds are bound together under the form of the Holy Body, and the worlds are associated together, and cohere together, and have been made one Body.[7]

1089. And since all things are one Body, the Schechinah Superior, the Schechinah Inferior—that Holy One, may He be blessed above! that Holy One, may He be blessed below!—hence is His Spirit drawn forth, and She entereth into the One Body, and in all things there appeareth nothing but the Unity.

1090. *Qadosh, Qadosh, Qadosh, Yod He Vau He Tzabaoth;* Holy, holy, holy, the Lord of the Hosts! the whole earth is full of Thy glory, for all things are Thy One Body.

1091. We have learned that because the one hath been tempered by the other, hence it is written, Cant. i, 11: "We will make thee borders of gold with studs of silver." For judgment and mercy are connected together (otherwise, judgment is tempered through mercy), and She is mitigated by Him.

1092. And therefore She ascendeth not without Him, like as with the palms; one sex ariseth not without the other.

1093. And therefore have we learned by tradition that if any one in this world cutteth himself off from the race of mankind, he hereafter, when he quitteth this world, shall not enter into the Syntagma of mankind, which is called the Holy Body; but (*shall enter*) among those who are not called mankind, so that he shall go forth from the Syntagma of the Body.

---

[7] "And they twain shall be one flesh."

1094. We have learned in exotic tradition that this is the sense of "We will make the borders of gold with studs of silver" (Cant. i, 11), that judgment is mitigated through mercy, so that there can be no judgment in which mercy is not found.

1095. And therefore it is written, *ibid.* 10: "Thy cheeks are beautiful in their outlines, and thy neck in pearls."

1096. "In outlines (or borders)," as it is written: "He will make thee borders of gold."

1097. "In pearls," answering to that which is written: "With studs of silver."

1098. "Thy neck" involveth the perfection of the Woman. This is found to be the habitation of the Sanctuary above, but the Jerusalem below.

1099. And all this is after that She is mitigated through the Male, and They twain are become one being, even the Syntagma of Truth.

1100. What is this Truth? Wherein is found all Truth?

1101. Thus have we learned. If any one be called Adam, and his soul (*Neschamah*) goeth from him, and he dieth, it is forbidden to leave him in his abode so that he should abide upon the earth.

1102. On account of the honor of that Body wherein no corruption can appear.

1103. For it is written, Ps. xlix, 13: "Man (*Adam*) shall not abide in honor;" that is, Adam, who is more worthy than all honor, shall not abide.

1104. Wherefore? Because if it were thus, he would be like unto the beasts (*Behemoth*) which perish.

1105. In what manner is it with the beast? He is not in the race of Adam, neither is he able to receive the Holy Spirit (RVChA QDIShA), for thus also would he be like unto the beast were his body without the Spirit, when at the same time that body (*of his*), which is the most honorable of all (*bodies, seeing it is the image of the Supernal*), is not meet to be associated with those things which are ignominious.

1106. Also we have learned in the "Book of Concealed Mystery," that were any one permitted to remain in such (*image of the*) Holy Body, and yet without the Spirit (*Ruacha*), there would be a void in the World.

1107. For assuredly, therefore, it could not be permitted unto him that he should abide in the holy place, in that earth wherein justice abideth. (Otherwise: Under the command of the Holy Crown, *Kether*, of the King, *Microprosopus*, in the earth, concerning which it is written, Isa. i, 21, "Justice abideth in Her.")

1108.[8] Since that venerable Body is the Form of the King; but if it were thus permitted to remain, then it would be counted as one of the beasts. (Otherwise: Since this venerable Body is called the Form of the King, and if it were thus left abiding, it would be like as the beast.) Therefore is it said, "Like unto the beasts which perish."

1109. We have learned this which is written, Gen. vi, 2: "And the sons of the Elohim beheld the daughters of Adam." These (*sons of the Elohim*) are they who were withdrawn, and who fell into the mouth of the Great Abyss.[9]

1110. "The daughters of Adam." (*Here it is to be noted that it is written Ha-Adam, the initial being demonstrative and emphatic, signifying*) of that especial Adam.

1111. And it is written: "And they came in unto them . . . the same were mighty men, who were from the Earth," etc. From that place, namely, which is called the earth, like as

---

[8] These sections are going on the idea of the Body remaining alive when the Divine Spirit has been withdrawn therefrom; that is, were it possible for it to be so.

[9] See *ante*, § 1048.

the tradition is concerning the phrase *Yemi Olahm*, the day of the world.

1112. The impurities[10] of the Name. From them have gone forth the Spirits, *Ruachin*, and the Demons, *Shedin*, into the world, so that they may adhere unto the wicked.

1113. "There were, *Ha-Nephilim*, Giants, *Be-Aretz*, in the earth"; for the restraining of those who were left, who existed not in the earth.

1114. Those giants are *Auza* and *Auzael*, who were in the earth, the sons of the Elohim were not in the earth. And this is an Arcanum, and all these things are said.

1115. It is written, Gen. vi, 6: "And it repented the Lord that He had formed Adam in the earth"; *i.e.*, for the restriction of the Supernal Adam, who is not in the earth.

1116. "And it repented the Lord"; this is said concerning Microprosopus.

1117. "And He was grieved about His heart"; it is not written, *Va-Yautzeb*, and He affected with grief; but *Va-Yethautzeb*, and He was touched with grief; *i.e.*, He was affected with grief from whom the matter depended, for the restriction of Him who was not touched with grief.

1118. "About His heart." It is not written, "within His heart," but "about His heart"; like as when any man is afflicted with grief, and mourneth before his Lord; for herein it is referred unto the heart of all hearts.

1119. And the Lord said: "I will destroy the Adam whom I have created, from off the face of *Ha-Adamah*, the Earth," etc., for the restriction[11] of the Adam, who is supernal.

1120. And if thou sayest that the Inferior Adam is alone to be understood, it is to be known that these cannot alto-

[10] Knorr von Rosenroth translates this word *Aneshi; Viri*, "men"; but I think "impurities" preferable.

[11] Or counterbalancing.

gether be opposed, seeing that the one existeth not without the other.

1121. And unless *Chokmah*, Wisdom, could be hidden from all, all things could be conformed like as from the beginning.

1122. Hence it is said, Prov. viii, 12: *"And Chokmah, I, Wisdom, have dwelt with Prudence"*; read it not *Shekenethi*, I have dwelt; but *Shikeneth-i*, My Shechinah or my Presence.

1123. And unless Adam were thus, the world could not consist; like as it is written, Prov. iii, 19: "The Lord in Chokmah hath founded the earth, *Tetragrammaton Be-Chokmah Yesed Areiz."*

1124. Also it is written, Gen. vi, 8: "And Noah found grace in the eyes of the Lord."

1125. Also we have learned that all brains depend from this brain (*supernal*).

1126. And *Chokmah*, Wisdom, also is a general name, but this concealed Wisdom corroborateth and conformeth the form of the Man, so that He may abide in his place.

1127. Like as it is written, Eccl. vii, 19: "Wisdom is a strength to a wise man more than ten rulers which are in a city"; which (*ten*) are the integral conformation of the man.

1128. Adam, truly, is the interior conformation, wherein consisteth the *Ruach*, Spirit; like as it is said, 1 Sam. xvi, 6: "Because Adam seeth according to the eyes, but the Lord seeth according to the heart," which is within the interior parts.

1129. And in that formation appeareth the true perfection of all things, which existeth above the Throne. Like as it is written: "And the appearance as the likeness of Adam upon it from above" (Ezek. i, 26).

1130. Also it is written, Dan. vii, 13: "And, behold, there came with the clouds of heaven one like unto a son of man, and even unto the Ancient of Days he came, and they made Him approach unto Him."

CHAPTER XLV[1]

CONCLUSION

1131. HEREUNTO are the concealed words, and the more secret meaning (*of them hath been set forth in many places*). Blessed is his portion who hath known and beheld them, and who erreth not therein.

1132. Because these words are not given forth save unto the Lords of Lords and the Reapers of the Field, who have both entered into and departed therefrom.

1133. Like as it is written, Hosea xiv, 9: "For the paths of the Lord are right, and the just shall walk in them, but transgressors shall fall therein."

1134. This have we learned. Rabbi Schimeon wept, and lifted up his voice and said: "If on account of our words which be here revealed, the Companions are to be concealed in the Conclave of the world to come, and are to be taken away from this world, it is justly and rightly done, in order that they may not reveal (*these secrets*) unto one of the children of this world."

1135. Again he said: "I return unto myself. For truly I have revealed (*these secrets*) before the Ancient of the Ancient Ones, the Concealed One with all Concealments; but not for mine own glory, not for the glory of the house of my father, not for the glory of these my Companions, have I done (*this thing*).

---

[1] It is worthy of note that the total number of chapters in the "Idra Rabba Qadisha" is 45, which is equal to MH, *Mah*, the concealed name of Yetzirah.

1136. "But in order that they might not err in His paths, nor that they might enter into the portals of His Palace to be made ashamed, nor that they might be destroyed for their error. Blessed be my portion with them in the world to come."

1137. We have learned that before the companions departed from this Assembly, Rabbi Yosi, Rabbi Chizqiah, and Rabbi Yisa died.

1138. And the companions beheld that the holy angels carried them away into that veil expanded above. And Rabbi Schimeon spake a certain word, and fell upon his face.

1139. Rabbi Schimeon cried aloud and said: "Wherefore is this? Because a certain decree hath been decreed against us to punish us, seeing that through us that hath been revealed which had not been revealed hitherto, from that day wherein Moses stood Upon the mountain of Sinai.

1140. "Like as it is written, Exod. xxxiv, 28: 'And he was there with the Lord forty days and forty nights.' Why then do I tarry here, if therefore I am to be punished?"

1141. And a Voice was heard which spake, and said: "Blessed art thou, Rabbi Schimeon, and blessed is thy portion, and that of those companions who are with thee; for unto ye hath that been revealed which is not revealed unto the whole supernal host.

1142. "But come, behold. It is written, Josh. vi, 26: 'And in his first-born son shall he establish it, and in his youngest son shall he set up the gates thereof'; much more than in this instance also are these taken away, seeing that with most severe and vehement study have they applied their souls (*Nepheschethhun*) hereunto at this time.

1143. "Blessed is their portion, for assuredly they have been taken away in perfection; and such were not those who were before them."

1144. Wherefore died they? We have learned this. When thus far these words were revealed, the Supernals and Inferiors of those Chariots were disturbed, and the Voice which revealed the Ancient Word below resounded through two hundred and fifty worlds.

1145. And before that those (three *Rabbis*) could recollect their souls, *Neschamathiyehu*, among those words (*of that Voice*) their souls had gone forth with a kiss;[2] and were joined unto that expanded veil, and the Supernal Angels carried them away.

1146. But wherefore those? Because they had entered in, and had not gone forth alternately, before this time. But all the others had entered in, and had gone forth.

1147. Rabbi Schimeon spake and said: "How blessed is the portion of those three, and therefore also blessed is our portion!"

1148. And a second time that Voice pealed forth and said, Deut. iv, 4: "But ye that did cleave unto the Lord, your God, are alive every one of you this day."

1149. They arose, and behold there was no place whence a fragrance went not forth.

1150. Rabbi Schimeon spake and said: "From this I perceive that the world receiveth blessing on account of us."

1151. And the faces of them all shone, so that men could not look upon them.

1152. We have learned that there were ten (*Rabbis*) entered into (*the Assembly*), and that seven came forth.

1153. And Rabbi Schimeon rejoiced, and Rabbi Abba was sad.

---

[2] The palace which is situated in the secret and most elevated part of heaven is called the Palace of Love. There dwells the Heavenly King— blessed be He!—with the holy souls, and is united with them with a loving kiss. This kiss is the union of the soul with the substance from which it emanated.

1154. On a certain day Rabbi Schimeon sat, and Rabbi Abba with him. Rabbi Schimeon spake a certain word.

1155. And they saw those three (*Rabbis*) who had died, and with them were most beautiful angels, who were showing unto them the supernal treasures and conclaves, on account of their great dignity.

1156. And they were entering into a mountain of pure balm; and the soul of Rabbi Abba was comforted.

1157. We have learned that after that day the companions did not quit the house of Rabbi Schimeon.

1158. And when Rabbi Schimeon revealed the Arcana, there were found none present there save those (*companions*).

1159. And Rabbi Schimeon called them the seven eyes of the Lord, like as it is written, Zach. iii, 9: "These are the seven eyes of the Lord." And this was said concerning us.[3]

1160. Rabbi Abba spake and said: "We six are lights which shine forth from a seventh (*light*); thou art the seventh light (*the origin of*) us all.

1161. "For assuredly there is no stability in those six, save (*what they derive*) from the seventh. For all things depend from the seventh."

1162. Rabbi Yehudah called him[4] the Sabbath of all the six (*Rabbi*).

1163. Like as it is written: "The Sabbath for the Lord, holy unto the Lord."

1164. What is the Sabbath? Holy unto the Lord; so also Rabbi Schimeon is, like the Sabbath, holy unto the Lord.

---

[3] Meaning, I suppose, that Rabbi Abba adds this by way of note to the text.

[4] Him: *i.e.,* Rabbi Schimeon Ben Yochai, who was chief among the seven surviving Rabbis, like the Sabbath among the days of the week.

1165. Rabbi Schimeon said: "It is strange that he[5] who is girded about the loins, and clothed with a heavy garment, was not found in the place of our conclave when those holy matters were revealed!"

1166. Meanwhile Elihu entered, and three beams of light shone in his countenance.

1167. Rabbi Schimeon said unto him: "Why was it that he was not present (otherwise, Why was not my lord present) in the sculptured square of his Lord in the nuptial day?"

1168. He answered unto him: "Through thy life, Rabbi, seven were chosen before Him, the Holy One—may He be blessed!—(otherwise, seven days are prostrate before the blessed God) all those who could come and abide with Him, before that ye could enter into the House of Conclave.

1169. "And I prayed that I might come among the others, and I wished to adhere unto His shoulders (otherwise, And I asked Him, that it might be permitted me to enter in, but He constrained my shoulders), and I could not.

1170. "For in that day was I sent that I might perform miracles for Rav Hamenuna the elder and his companions, who had been taken away into the palace (otherwise: into the prison) of the King.

1171. "And I performed a miracle for them, and cast down the King's rampart (otherwise: I cast down the wall of the royal palace for them), with whose chains they were bound; so that (their) forty-five warders were kept back.

1172. "And I led forth Rav Hamenuna and his companions, and brought them up unto the valley of Aunu; and they have been set free.

1173. "And I have given unto them bread and water, seeing they had not eaten for three days.

---

[5] Elihu, who now enters.

1174. "And all the day I quitted them not.

1175. "And when I returned (*hither*), I found the Veil expanded, which all these Columns[6] upheld; and three of the Companions (*had ascended*) above it.

1176. "And I spake unto them, and they answered: 'This is the portion of God the most Holy One—may He be blessed!—from the nuptials[7] of Rabbi Schimeon and his companions.'

1177. "Blessed art thou, Rabbi Schimeon, and blessed is thy portion, and that of those companions who are sitting in thy presence.

1178. "How many paths are prepared for ye in the world to come! how many lights of lights are prepared that they may enlighten ye!

1179. "And come, behold! Therefore on this day there are bound together for thee fifty crowns for Rabbi Benchas Ben Yair, thy father-in-law, and I walk with him.

1180. "And all those are rivers of the mountains of pure balm, for assuredly his place and lot is chosen (otherwise: and I saw that he had, etc.)."

1181. (*Rabbi Schimeon*) said unto him: "Are therefore the just united by the Union of the Diadems more on the days of the New Moon, of the feasts, and of the Sabbaths, than on any other days?"

1182. He answered unto him: "Most certainly; also all those who are without. Like as it is written, Isa. lxvi, 23: 'And it shall come to pass that from one new moon to another, and from one sabbath unto another, shall all flesh come to worship before me, saith the Lord.'

1183. "If those come, how much more the just!

[6] The columns of the Sephiroth.

[7] This term is occasionally used in a mystical sense to signify the acquisition of divine wisdom.

1184. "Wherefore from one new moon unto another? Because the patriarchs surround the Holy Chariot.

1185. "And from one Sabbath unto another Sabbath, because the seventh day is surrounded by all the other six days.

1186. "Like as it is written: 'And the Elohim blessed the seventh day,' etc.

1187. "And thou, Rabbi Schimeon, art the seventh: thou shalt be the chief; and thou shalt be more crowned and sanctified than all.

1188. "And with three most delicious feasts of the seventh day shall the just be entertained because of thee in the world to come.

1189. "Also it is written, Isa. lviii, 13: 'Thou shalt call the sabbath a delight, the holy of the Lord, honorable.'

1190. "Who is He, the Holy One of the Lord? This is Rabbi Schimeon Ben Yochai, who is called very glorious (*both*) in this world and in (*the world*) to come."

Hereunto is the Greater Holy Assembly.